D0976024

09   10
     11

11/01
1

Biology!
BEST
SCIENCE
PROJECTS

Cell and Microbe Science Fair Projects

Using Microscopes, Mold, and More

Kenneth G. Rainis

Enslow Publishers, Inc.

40 Industrial Road	PO Box 38
Box 398	Aldershot
Berkeley Heights, NJ 07922	Hants GU12 6BP
USA	UK

http://www.enslow.com

In memory of my boyhood best friend,
Brian Fusco—
one of a kind and taken too early.

Acknowledgments

This book would not have become a reality without the loving support of my wife, Joan. Thanks to my partners at Neo/SCI—Kurt Gelke, Jean Coniber, and George Nassis—whose support is greatly appreciated. Special thanks to Ken Rando, who, as always, helped with the electrons.

Library of Congress Cataloging-in-Publication Data

Rainis, Kenneth G.
Cell and microbe science fair projects using microscopes, mold, and more /
Kenneth G. Rainis.
p. cm. — (Biology! best science projects)
Includes index.
ISBN 0-7660-2369-9 (hardcover)
1. Cytology—Juvenile literature. 2. Microbiology—Juvenile literature.
3. Microscopy—Juvenile literature. 4. Biology projects—Juvenile literature.
I. Title. II. Series.
QH582.5.R35 2005
571.6'0078—dc22

                                                            2004015720

Printed in the United States of America

10 9 8 7 6 5 4 3 2 1

To Our Readers: We have done our best to make sure all Internet Addresses in this book were active and appropriate when we went to press. However, the author and the publisher have no control over and assume no liability for the material available on those Internet sites or on other Web sites they may link to. Any comments or suggestions can be sent by e-mail to comments@enslow.com or to the address on the back cover.

Illustration Credits: Kenneth G. Rainis, pp. 17, 28, 34, 42, 59, 65, 77, 87, 93, 96, 101, 110, 115–121; Neo/SCI Corporation, Rochester, New York, pp. 11, 12, 15, 21, 22, 23, 40, 45, 51, 55, 70, 71.

Cover Illustration Credits: © 2002–2003 ArtToday, Inc. (8, 9); © 2005 JupiterImages Corporation (girl); Copyright © Dennis Kunkel Microscopy, Inc. (1, 2, 3, 4, 5, 6); Kenneth G. Rainis (background, 7).

| 1 | 2 | 3 | 4 | 5 | 6 | 7 | 8 | 9 |

Contents

Chapter 1

Getting to Know Cells

The human body contains over 75 trillion cells. However, most life-forms on Earth exist as single cells that perform all the functions necessary for them to live on their own. Most cells are far too small to be seen with the naked eye. High-power microscopes are needed to carefully examine them.

Until the mid-seventeenth century, scientists did not know that cells even existed. It wasn't until 1665 that English scientist Robert Hooke (1635–1703) observed through his microscope that plant tissues were divided into tiny compartments, which he called cellulae, or cells (see Figure 1). It took another 175 years before scientists began to understand the true importance of cells. In their studies of plant and animal cells during the early nineteenth century, German botanist Matthias Schleiden (1804–1881) and German zoologist Theodor Schwann (1810–1882) recognized the fundamental "sameness" between the two cell types acknowledged at the time—plant and animal. In 1838, they proposed the cell theory—all living things are made up of one or more cells. This theory, now accepted by most scientists, also says that cells are the basic units of structure and function; and that cells are produced from existing cells. The

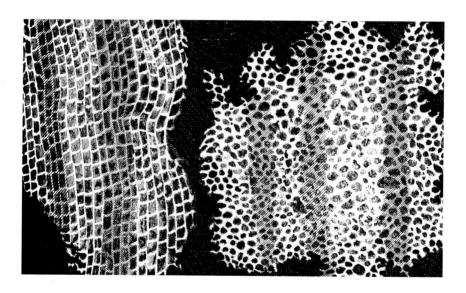

Figure 1.

This figure was published in *Micrographia* (1665). Robert Hooke's illustration of thinly sectioned cork tissue shows the numerous "cells" first described by him.

investigations in this book will help you understand how cells function and the differences among them.

Microbes are very small, microscopic organisms. All microbes are made of cells. A French surgeon, Charles Sedillot (1848–1892), coined the term *microbe*. The term was first used in 1878 to describe the "whole body of infinitely small organisms." In this book, it refers to organisms too small to be seen in detail with the naked eye.

Some people believe that viruses are the smallest forms of life. Viruses are not alive. They behave as chemicals until they enter a cell. Inside a host cell, a virus takes over cellular machinery to reproduce itself. Cells, on the other hand, direct chemical reactions, grow, and make copies of themselves.

Since 1675, scientists have studied the natural world to observe, learn, and understand the ways in which cells and microbes live and reproduce. Let's begin our journey!

THE SCIENTIFIC METHOD

As a junior scientist, you will use instruments, including a microscope, to make careful observations. You will work out a reasoned guess (or hypothesis) to explain what you observed. You will design a method (an experiment) to test your hypothesis. Then you will use your results (data) to conclude whether your hypothesis was correct or whether it should be changed.

THE INVESTIGATIONS IN THIS BOOK

Each experiment in this book presents a question, which is answered by doing an investigation. In fact, some investigations are similar to the very ones microbiologists like Hooke, Robert Koch, and Pasteur made to learn more about cells and microbes. "Science Project Ideas" present open-ended suggestions for further investigation using the methods and information contained in the experiment. A unique feature of this book is "The Microbe Identification Guide" (Appendix A)—a resource for identifying microbes in various locations called microhabitats.

TOOLS YOU WILL NEED

Most of the items you will need for your investigations can be found around the house. Because most of the subjects of your studies are microscopic, you will need a microscope having at least 430X magnification. There are many inexpensive microscopes, including computer microscopes, available to you (see Appendix B). You may also be able to use a microscope with a very high magnification (960X) at school. Your science teacher is an excellent source for advice, as well as for laboratory equipment and chemicals. The most essential tool of science, of course, is your curiosity!

SAFETY FIRST

1. Be serious about science. A careless attitude can be dangerous to you and to others.

2. Never look into a lens pointed at the sun. Doing so can cause serious injury to your eyes.

3. Read instructions carefully before proceeding with any investigation outlined in this book. When expanding on these activities, discuss your experimental procedure with a knowledgeable adult before you begin.

4. Keep your work area clean and organized. Never drink or eat while conducting experiments.

5. Wear protective glasses when doing activities involving chemicals, when heating objects or water, or when performing any other experiment that could lead to eye injury.

6. Do not touch chemicals with your bare hands unless instructed to do so. Do not taste chemicals or chemical solutions. Do not inhale vapors or fumes from any chemical or chemical solution.

7. Clean up any chemical spill immediately. If you spill anything on your skin or clothing, rinse it off immediately with plenty of water. Then report what happened to a responsible adult.

8. Keep flammable liquids away from heat sources.

9. Always wash your hands before and after conducting activities. Dispose of contaminated waste or articles properly.

Chapter 2

Organisms and Their Cells

All known organisms can be placed into one of two large groups, depending on the types of cells of which they are made. Figure 2 shows examples from these two cell type groups. The first group is the prokaryotes. They have their genetic material (DNA) organized as a single, simple chromosome that floats about inside the cell. The second cell type group is the eukaryotes. Their DNA is organized into a number of complex chromosomes inside a membrane sac called a nucleus.

a) PROKARYOTIC CELL

bacteria cell

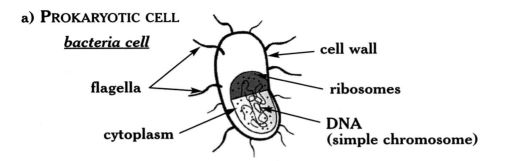

flagella

cytoplasm

cell wall

ribosomes

DNA
(simple chromosome)

b) EUKARYOTIC CELLS

plant cell

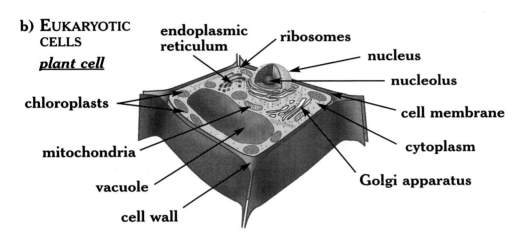

endoplasmic reticulum

ribosomes

nucleus

nucleolus

cell membrane

cytoplasm

Golgi apparatus

chloroplasts

mitochondria

vacuole

cell wall

animal cell

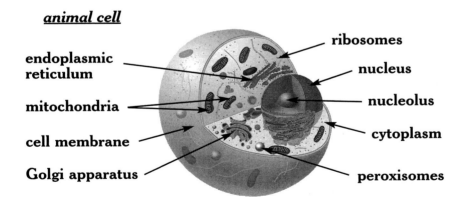

endoplasmic reticulum

mitochondria

cell membrane

Golgi apparatus

ribosomes

nucleus

nucleolus

cytoplasm

peroxisomes

Figure 2.

a) Prokaryotes (bacteria and cyanobacteria) have a simple DNA chromosome. b) Eukaryotic cells, such as this plant cell and animal cell, have complex chromosomes contained within a membrane-bound nucleus.

Scientists have arranged life-forms into large groupings, or kingdoms, based on their cell type and organization. See Table 1.

Table 1.

ORGANISMS AND THEIR CELLS

Kingdom	Cell Type	Cell Organization	
Bacteria	prokaryote	Single cells, sometimes living in groups (all unicellular)	
Protists (most are microscopic organisms)	eukaryote	Most are single cells; some live in groups called colonies (most unicellular)	
Fungi (molds, yeasts, and mushrooms)	eukaryote	Most are made up of many cells; some are single cells (most multicellular)	
Plants	eukaryote	Body is made of many cells that form tissues (all multicellular)	
Animals	eukaryote	Body is made of many cells that form tissues (all multicellular)	

A unicellular organism is a single cell. Other organisms, like the green protist *Volvox*, are made up of hundreds of similar cells living closely together—a colony. Organisms such as mushrooms, trees, and humans are multicellular. Multicellular organisms have a number of different kinds of cells. Each kind of cell (e.g., liver cell, muscle cell) has a certain role to play. In some multicellular organisms, cells of the same kind may be organized into groups called tissues that perform the same function.

Use Table 2 as a guide to some of the major differences between prokaryotic and eukaryotic cells. You will be exploring many of these cell characteristics in the investigations outlined in this book. Let's get to work!

Table 2.

COMPARISON OF PROKARYOTIC AND EUKARYOTIC CELLS

Characteristic	Prokaryotes	Eukaryotes
Size	Mostly small cells (1–10 μm)	Mostly large cells (10–100 μm)
DNA	Organized into a single, simple chromosome; not in a nucleus	Organized into many complex chromosomes within a nucleus
Multicellular Forms	Rare; no tissue development	Common; tissues develop
Cell Division	Mostly by cell fission (dividing in two)	Mostly by mitosis (the nucleus divides)
Organelles ("Little Organs")	None	Many types
Need for Oxygen	Can change	All need oxygen for life
Movement	Simple flagella	Complex flagella; other types
Note: A micrometer (μm) is 0.000001 meter or 1/25,000 inch.		

Investigation 1

Why Are Most Cells Small?

Materials

- ✓ **an adult**
- ✓ clear plastic metric ruler
- ✓ newsprint
- ✓ modeling clay
- ✓ plastic knife
- ✓ scissors
- ✓ hen's egg
- ✓ shallow dish
- ✓ water
- ✓ spiderwort flower with stamen hairs
- ✓ tweezers
- ✓ forceps
- ✓ eyedropper
- ✓ microscope slide
- ✓ coverslip
- ✓ compound microscope, with light source
- ✓ magnifying glass

Most eukaryote cells are only approximately 100 μm (micrometers) long. This means that 100 of these cells lined up end to end equal just one centimeter! Being able to determine the size of a cell or a cell structure is a very important skill. Let's practice on something a little larger than the average eukaryote cell—the dot of an *i*.

To measure objects with the microscope, you will need to know something called the field diameter. To measure the field diameter, place a clear, plastic metric ruler on the microscope

a)   Student Microscope

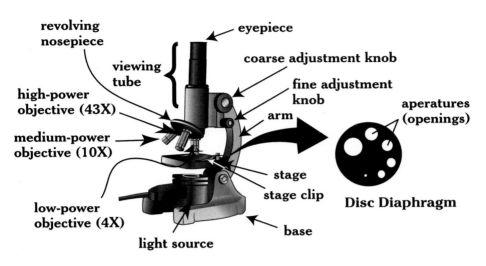

revolving nosepiece

eyepiece

viewing tube

coarse adjustment knob

high-power objective (43X)

fine adjustment knob

medium-power objective (10X)

aperatures (openings)

arm

low-power objective (4X)

stage

stage clip

Disc Diaphragm

base

light source

b)   Advanced Microscope

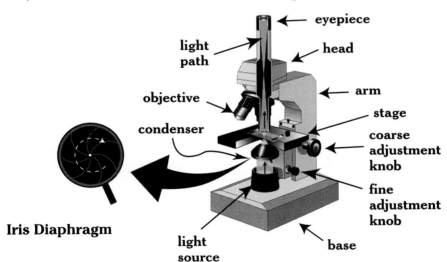

eyepiece

light path

head

objective

arm

condenser

stage

coarse adjustment knob

fine adjustment knob

Iris Diaphragm

light source

base

Figure 3.

a) This compound microscope is a student microscope with a disc diaphragm. b) This advanced microscope has an iris diaphragm. *Note:* These microscopes may have a mirror instead of a powered light source.

stage, securing it with the stage clips. Use Figure 3 as a guide to using the compound microscope. Turn on the microscope light, or adjust the mirror so that indirect sunlight (light from a window) is allowed to shine through the clear ruler. **NEVER use a microscope mirror to reflect direct sunlight—it could damage your eyes!**

If necessary, turn the revolving nosepiece to bring the 4X objective into position over the transparent ruler. You will feel a click as the new objective locks into place. While looking through the eyepiece, use the coarse focus adjustment knob to bring the field of view into focus at 40X magnification (4X objective and 10X eyepiece lens provides 40X total magnification). You should only have to use the fine adjustment knob, twisting it upward, to achieve a sharp focus. You should be able to observe an even, bright circle of light and sharp ruler markings.

Adjust the focus so that the scale is clearly in view at low magnification (40X). Line up the 1-cm mark with the very left edge of your field of view. In your notebook, record the distance from the left edge to the right edge; see Figure 4. The viewing area or field diameter at 40X magnification should be approximately 4 mm (4,000 μm) wide. Table 3 lists approximate field diameter measurements for various magnifications in a compound microscope.

4X Objective Field of View

Dot *i* Newsprint Character

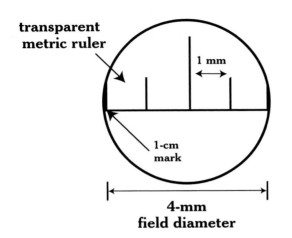

transparent
metric ruler

1 mm

1-cm
mark

4-mm
field diameter

Figure 4.

a) Measure the 4X objective field of view.
b) Dot on the *i* in newsprint.

Table 3.

FIELD DIAMETERS FOR VARIOUS MAGNIFICATIONS

Eyepiece Magnification	Objective Magnification	Field Diameter
10X	4X	4 mm (4,000 μm)
10X	10X	1.6 mm (1,600 μm)
10X	43X	0.37 mm (370 μm)
10X	96X	0.16 mm (160 μm)
Note: 1 mm = 1,000 μm		

Once you know the field diameter, you can easily estimate a viewed object's size. For example, if an object takes up three-fourths of a 1.6 mm field diameter, it would measure approximately 1.2 mm, or 1,200 μm.

Let's put your measuring skills to the test. Examine a piece of newsprint containing the letter *i*. Place the newsprint on the stage and center the line of type containing the *i* in the center of the hole in the stage. Rotate the 4X objective into place. Carefully focus until you can see a sharp image. Position the *i*'s dot so that it is in the center of your field of view. Can you determine the size of the *i*'s dot? Using the information in Table 2, how many bacteria, laid side by side, could fit across the dot of an *i*? How many eukaryotic cells?

But what limits the size of cells? Sometimes constructing models can help you visualize the relationships of size, surface area, and volume—critical factors in the life of a cell.

Many plant and animal cells are rectangular or cube-shaped. You can use modeling clay, a plastic knife, and a metric ruler to make models of cubic skin cells. Make one cube 1 cm long, 1 cm wide, and 1 cm high—about 1,000X bigger than an actual cell in your body. Next, construct another cube whose dimensions are four times larger—4 cm long, 4 cm wide, and 4 cm high.

Table 4 provides a summary of these cell model areas and volumes. These data will be helpful in explaining why, as cells grow, they must divide and stay small.

Table 4.

CALCULATING CELL SURFACE AREAS TO VOLUME

	Length (cm)	Width (cm)	Height (cm)	Surface Area (cm^2)	Volume (cm^3)	Ratio of Surface Area to Volume (SA:V)
Cell Model #1	1	1	1	6	1	6 : 1
Cell Model #2	4	4	4	96	64	1.5 : 1
Surface area (cm^2) = sum of the area of all sides. (A cube has 6 sides.) Volume (cm^3) = length × width × height						

As the data in Table 4 shows, volume and surface area do not increase by the same proportions. Volume increases more rapidly than surface area because volume is a measure of three dimensions (cm^3), while surface area measures only two dimensions (cm^2).

What does this mean for cells? All cells must be able to receive nutrients and get rid of wastes. If they cannot do these two tasks, they will die. The data in Table 4 show that less surface area is available for the passage of nutrients and wastes per unit volume in a larger cell than a smaller cell. Thus, small is more efficient! That is why most active cells are small.

Cheek cells are shaped like pancakes. Scientists classify these lining cells as squamous (flat). This cell type is found lining such structures as microscopic lung sacs called alveoli. Look at Figure 5a, a section of human lung tissue. Can you pick out lung sac cells?

Use the bar scale at the bottom of Figure 5b to measure and calculate the surface area and volume of another flat cell— a cheek cell. Do your observations and calculations tell you why this cell shape would tend to help things move into and out of the cell? Why do large, multicellular organisms, such as humans, need a circulatory system if all of our individual cells are small?

CELLS THAT YOU CAN SEE

Some types of cells, like egg cells, are not active. These inactive cells are usually much larger than most other cells. For example, a frog's egg (with a 1,500-μm diameter) is 15X larger than most cells.

Crack a hen's egg and place it in a shallow dish for you to examine. Measure the egg cell. How much larger is it compared to a common eukaryote cell? What is it mostly made of? Reptile and bird eggs are large because the developing young need food (yolk) to grow outside the mother's body.

Examine another large cell, a stamen hair cell, in a spiderwort plant. You can buy a blooming spiderwort plant from a local florist or commercial grower. Use a magnifying glass to look at the tiny hairs in the center of the flower. Under the magnifier, the hair looks like tiny beads

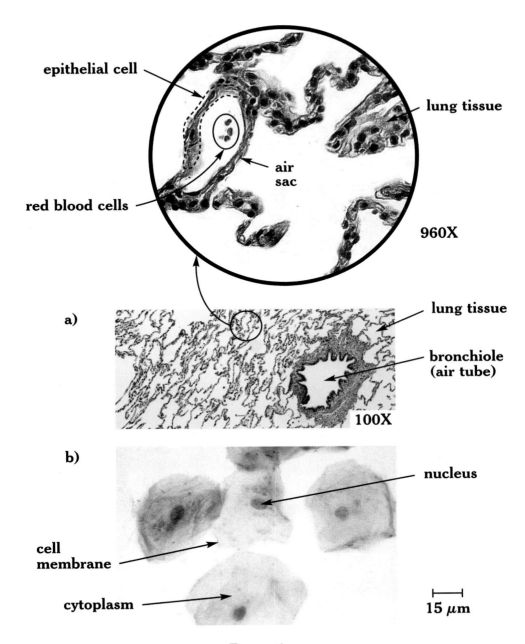

epithelial cell

lung tissue

red blood cells

air sac

960X

a)

lung tissue

bronchiole (air tube)

100X

b)

nucleus

cell membrane

cytoplasm

15 μm

Figure 5.

a) Human lung tissue at 100X showing a bronchiole (air tube), and a highly magnified view (960X) showing a microscopic air sac made up of several cells. Use the bar scale to measure one of the cells. b) A stained cheek cell. Use the bar scale to measure its size.

stacked on top of one another. Each of these beads is a hair cell. Use tweezers to remove a single stamen hair and place it in a drop of water on a microscope slide. Complete a wet mount preparation (see Figure 6) by adding a coverslip. Examine the slide under a compound microscope, first at low magnification (40X), then at higher magnifications. Be sure to adjust the iris or disc diaphragm to not allow too much light to pass through the sample. Measure a stamen hair cell. Is it larger than the dot of an *i*? Why do you suppose it is so large?

a) b)

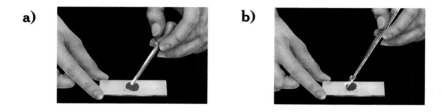

Figure 6.

MAKING A WET MOUNT PREPARATION

a) Place the specimen in a drop of water on a clean microscope slide.
b) Use forceps to hold the coverslip. Carefully drop the coverslip onto the water drop and specimen to complete the wet mount preparation.

Science Project Idea

U se the bar scale to calculate the surface area and volume of the human epithelial cells in Figure 7. Compare these data to your calculations for the cheek cells shown in Figure 5b. Do your calculations help to explain why some medicines are applied directly onto the gums or skin?

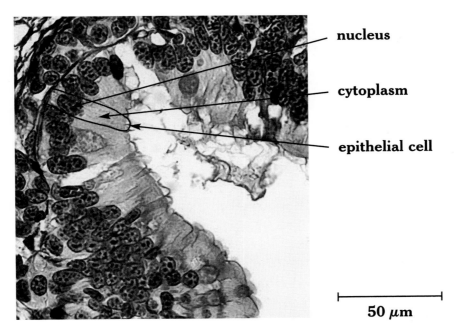

nucleus

cytoplasm

epithelial cell

50 μm

Figure 7.

Epithelial cells are covering cells: They make tissues that cover surfaces. Use the bar scale to measure the size of some of them.

Investigation 2

What Makes a Prokaryote?

Materials

- ✓ **an adult**
- ✓ collected cyanobacteria
- ✓ watertight container
- ✓ penknife
- ✓ toothpicks
- ✓ microscope slides
- ✓ coverslips
- ✓ forceps
- ✓ 0.1% crystal violet or 0.1% methylene blue stain
- ✓ safety glasses
- ✓ disposable gloves
- ✓ paper cup
- ✓ clothespin
- ✓ 2 eyedroppers
- ✓ cup filled with water
- ✓ compound microscope, with light source

Safety: Have an adult present and use care when working with biological stains. Avoid skin and eye contact. Wear safety glasses and disposable gloves.

Bacteria are prokaryotes. The structure of a prokaryotic cell is simple. It is essentially a bag of fluid (cytoplasm) with DNA and other small bodies floating about. This fluid and its contents are usually contained within a sturdy cell wall. What bacteria lack in structural complexity, they more than make up for in chemistry, as you will learn!

CYANOBACTERIA

Cyanobacteria are very large, colored prokaryotic cells. The single cells are arranged in either threadlike filaments or are scattered about in a clear, round, gel-like material called coccoids. Use "The Microbe Identification Guide" (Appendix A) to help you identify these common colored bacteria.

Most cyanobacteria make their own food through photosynthesis. They use the sun's energy to convert carbon dioxide (CO_2) and water (H_2O) to oxygen (O_2) and sugars (carbohydrates) that they use for food. Photosynthetic pigments scattered throughout the cell give them a blue-black or blue-green color.

Cyanobacteria can be found in almost any aquatic (watery) environment. Some cyanobacteria form dark films or scums that are often quite slippery when exposed on wet rocks along a shoreline. If possible, remove a small stone covered with a blue-green film of cyanobacteria and place it in a container of collected or bottled water to bring back to your lab. You can also use a penknife to take scrapings from rocks and mix them with a small quantity of collected water in a container.

Once in your lab, you will make a wet mount preparation. Use a toothpick to mix a small amount of collected cyanobacteria with a drop of water on a clean microscope slide. Use forceps to hold the coverslip. Carefully drop the coverslip onto the water drop and specimen to complete the wet mount preparation (see Figure 6). Avoid creating bubbles; they can hamper your microscopic observations.

Using the low-power (4X) objective allows you to scan the sample because it provides the largest field of view. Carefully move the slide around to scan for an interesting group of threadlike filaments or groups of green cells inside a clear gel (coccoids) to examine. Adjust the iris or disc diaphragm for the best lighting that allows you to see crisp images. You will need more light (a wider diaphragm opening) at higher magnifications.

To switch to a higher magnification, carefully turn the nosepiece and bring the next higher power objective (10X) into position over your sample. **Remember: Never focus downward; it could drive the objective into your preparation and damage it and the objective!**

Can you observe the individual cells that make up the filaments or coccoids? Now switch to high magnification (430X) by rotating the 43X objective into place to observe individual filament cells closely. Can you see any cell organelles such as green chloroplasts or nuclei? Or do you observe cells each having an overall blue-green color without cell organelles? Compare your microscopic observations to Figure 2a and Tables 1 and 2. Use "The Microbe Identification Guide" (Appendix A) to help you identify collected cyanobacteria and other prokaryotes.

BACTERIA

Bacteria are prokaryotes. They are tiny rods, spheres, and spirals. Probably the first observations of bacteria were made by Dutch cloth merchant, Antoni van Leeuwenhoek (1632–1723). Here is his description of his own tooth plaque:

> *Tho my teeth are kept unusually very clean, nevertheless when I view them in a Magnifying Glass, I find growing between them a little white matter as thick as wetted flower: in this substance tho I do not perceive any motion, I judged there might probably be live creatures.*

> —Antoni van Leeuwenhoek
> September 17, 1683

Can you find prokaryotes in your tooth plaque? Use a clean toothpick to scrape plaque from your teeth. Use Figure 8 as a guide in making a stain smear preparation. Mix the plaque with a drop of water on a microscope slide. Then use the toothpick to spread out the drop on the slide. Allow the smear to air dry. Use a clothespin to hold the slide over a paper cup. Collect some 0.1% crystal violet or 0.1% methylene blue stain (see your science teacher) with an eyedropper and flood the smear on the slide by allowing drops to pile up, creating a single large drop. Let the stain sit on the slide for two to three minutes.

Use another eyedropper to apply single drops of water to rinse the stain off the slide into a paper cup. Allow the stained slide to air dry. Examine the slide under 430X (or a higher magnification if you can). Use "The Microbe Identification Guide"

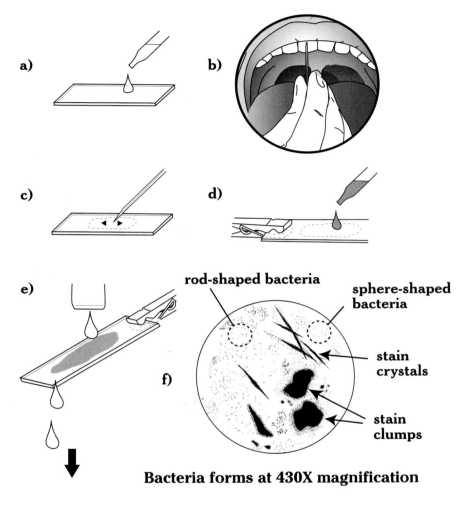

a) b) c) d)

e)

f)

rod-shaped bacteria

sphere-shaped bacteria

stain crystals

stain clumps

Bacteria forms at 430X magnification

Figure 8.

MAKING A STAINED SMEAR

a) Add a drop of water to a clean slide. b) Use a toothpick or cotton applicator to scrape a surface to collect bacteria. c) Mix the scraping with the drop of water and allow to dry. d) Add a drop or two of stain; wait two or three minutes. e) Rinse using drops of water. f) Observe under a compound microscope.

(Appendix A) to help you identify the types of bacteria that reside in your mouth. Can you observe rods or spheres?

Use Investigation 1 as a guide in estimating the size of observed stained tooth plaque bacteria and cyanobacteria cells. Do your data agree with those presented in Table 2?

Record your microscopic observations (including drawings) in your notebook. How do your drawings of stained plaque bacteria compare with those Leeuwenhoek submitted in his letter to the Royal Society in London in 1683, shown in Figure 9?

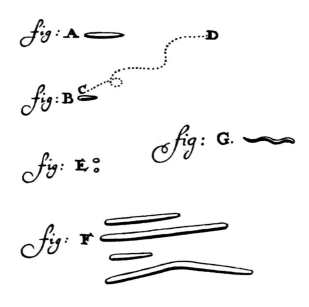

Figure 9.

This illustration by Leeuwenhoek shows the major bacteria forms from Leeuwenhoek's mouth: rod (bacillus; A, B, and F), sphere (coccus; E), and spiral (spirillum; G).

Science Project Idea

How common are prokaryotes that you can see with your eye? Are certain prokaryotes, such as cyanobacteria, some of the most common of visible microbes? Travel to aquatic environments **with an adult** and look around. Keep a journal of your travels and observations. You may wish to take samples for microscopic study back to the lab with you. Transport wet material, along with water collected at the scene, in watertight containers. Suggested locations (microhabitats) to scout include:

- Damp, shaded stone structures such as fountains, sidewalks, and pavement curbs. Look for a light blue-green coloration. Take scrapings and examine under the microscope at 430X magnification. (Grass-green coloration usually indicates growing eukaryote cells [algae].)

- Colored mats on submerged aquatic plants, brightly colored mud on damp soil and rocks.

- Stromatolites—fossilized cyanobacteria mats that are 500 million to billions of years old. A quite accessible site is in Ballston Spa, New York (at the Petrified Sea Gardens). Many local museums have stromatolite collections as well.

Investigation 3

What Makes a Eukaryote?

Materials

- ✓ **an adult**
- ✓ kitchen knife
- ✓ red onion
- ✓ 3 eyedroppers
- ✓ microscope slides
- ✓ tweezers
- ✓ iodine or 0.1% methylene blue stain
- ✓ water
- ✓ disposable gloves
- ✓ safety glasses
- ✓ forceps
- ✓ coverslips
- ✓ *Elodea* leaf
- ✓ toothpick, flat-ended
- ✓ compound microscope, with light source

Safety: Have an adult present and use care when working with biological stains. Avoid skin and eye contact. Wear safety glasses and disposable gloves.

The structure of a eukaryotic cell is far more complex than a prokaryotic cell. The DNA is packaged in a number of complex chromosomes inside a membrane sac, forming the nucleus. Floating in the cytoplasm along with the nucleus are other membrane-surrounded little organs called organelles.

Except for bacteria, all other life-forms—fungi, protists, plants, and animals—have a nucleus. Let's examine the cells of different life-forms up close.

EXAMINING PLANT CELLS

Although the fleshy part of an onion grows underground, it is actually made of leaves. These leaves are thick because they store food for the plant. The very thin layers of covering cells on the leaf surfaces are called the skin. **Ask an adult** to cut up a red onion into wedge-shaped pieces. Examine a piece of the cut onion and break it apart to expose a single leaf.

Can you confirm that an onion leaf is made up of eukaryotic cells? Use an eyedropper to place a drop of water in the center of a glass microscope slide. Use tweezers to remove the thin tissue layer from the thicker part of the leaf. Place the piece of onion skin in the drop of water on the microscope slide. Add another drop of water or a contrast stain such as 0.1% methylene blue (or iodine stain if available) over the onion epidermis and finish making a wet mount by adding a coverslip (see Figure 6). The iodine or 0.1% methylene blue stain will color structures inside the cell, giving them extra contrast so that they will be more visible.

Begin by examining the preparation at low magnification (40X). You may need to reduce the lighting by using the disc or iris diaphragm.

Switch to 100X magnification. Using Figure 2 as a guide, can you find a cell nucleus or other cell structures in onion leaf cells? Estimate the size (length and width) of these onion cells at various magnification levels (100X and 430X). Record your observations and measurements in your notebook. How does your field of view compare to Figure 10a? Does your measurement data support the statement in Table 2 that bacteria cells (prokaryotes) are generally smaller than onion cells (eukaryotes)?

CHECKING OUT CHLOROPLASTS

Another organelle inside some eukaryotic cells is the plastid. Like the nucleus, a plastid is an organelle and also has a membrane that surrounds it. Plastids occur in all plant cells. They are also found in certain protist cells. (Remember, protists are one-celled organisms. An organism is any living creature, either single-celled or multicelled.) Plastids contain pigments. The most common example of a plastid is the chloroplast that contains chlorophyll for photosynthesis.

Chloroplasts are fairly large organelles. You can view them easily in the aquarium plant *Elodea*. Obtain *Elodea* at a pet or aquarium store. Use tweezers to remove a leaf from the growing tip of the plant. Make a wet mount (see Figure 6) by placing the leaf in a drop of water on a clean microscope slide. Add a coverslip and examine first at low magnification (40X), then at higher magnifications. Be sure to adjust the iris or disc diaphragm to allow enough light to pass through the leaf. Carefully focus on a single *Elodea* cell. Compare your field of view with Figure 10b.

Can you see small, green, oval-shaped chloroplasts inside an *Elodea* cell? How large are they? Use Figure 10 as a guide in identifying other internal eukaryotic structures in onion and *Elodea*. Are the chloroplasts found in one area of the cell, or are they scattered about?

a)

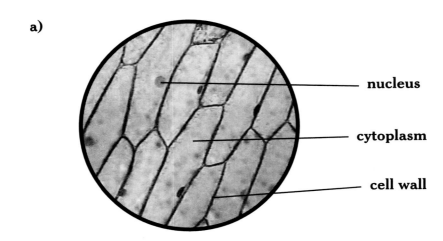

nucleus

cytoplasm

cell wall

b)

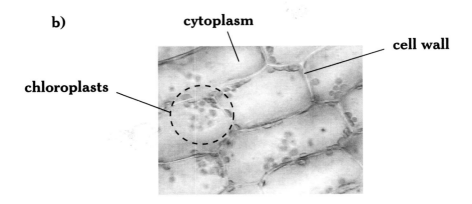

cytoplasm

cell wall

chloroplasts

Figure 10.
a) **Onion cells at 430X. b)** *Elodea* **leaf cells at 960X.**

EXAMINING ANIMAL CELLS

The lining of the inside of your mouth is made of a layer of pancake-like epithelial cells. **Under adult supervision**, use a flat-ended toothpick to carefully and gently scrape the inside of your cheek to collect some cheek epithelial cells.

Mix the scraped cells in a drop of either iodine or 0.1% methylene blue stain on a clean glass microscope slide. Rinse and complete the wet mount preparation (see Figure 6) by adding a coverslip. Examine the preparation first at low magnification (40X), then at higher magnifications. Be sure to adjust the iris or disc diaphragm to not allow too much light to pass through the sample. Carefully focus on a single stained cheek cell. Examine your cheek cells closely. Can you locate the cell's nucleus? Does your cheek cell contain any plastids?

Measure the size of these cells. Does your measurement data support the statement that plant and animal cells are about the same size? Are prokaryotic cells generally smaller than eukaryotic cells?

Science Project Idea

Have an adult help you obtain a pondwater or puddle water sample. Expect to find many kinds of eukaryotic cells—single cells and cells grouped together (colonies). Many protists move quickly, making them hard to study. You will need to add a barrier that will slow them down without harming them. The slowing solution will enable you to view cell movement and internal cell functions more easily. To make a protist-slowing solution, thoroughly mix 1 teaspoon of polyethylene oxide (see Appendix C) in 3 ounces (90 mL) of warm water. Stir the mixture continually with a wooden craft stick to make sure all the polyethylene oxide goes into solution. Use a toothpick to pick up a small amount of this solution and transfer it to a clean microscope slide. Then add a drop of pondwater to the solution. Mix the two drops with a toothpick. Add a coverslip to complete the wet mount preparation (see Figure 6).

Examine the pondwater preparation first at low magnification (40X), then at higher magnifications (100X and 430X). Be sure to adjust the iris or disc diaphragm to not allow too much light to pass through the sample. Try to locate a single large cell, such as a ciliate—a protist that moves about using fine hairlike structures called cilia. Use

"The Microbe Identification Guide" (Appendix A) to help you identify ciliates and other kinds of protists you find.

Using Figure 2 and Table 2, try to answer these questions: How are large pond ciliate cells similar to or different from cheek cells? Onion cells? What organelles are common to all eukaryotic cells you have observed?

Measure these pond cell organisms. How does the size of a large ciliate cell compare in size with other eukaryote cells you have observed (onion and cheek)?

Based on your observations, are some cell types more specialized than others? How so? Investigation 4 will help you answer these questions.

Investigation 4

Are All Eukaryote Cells the Same?

Materials

- ✓ **an adult**
- ✓ animal meat—heart and muscle (from a grocery store or butcher)
- ✓ 0.1% methylene blue stain
- ✓ disposable gloves
- ✓ safety glasses
- ✓ soft plant tissues: celery, broccoli, tomato, carrot, potato, other stems and roots

- ✓ water
- ✓ microscope slides
- ✓ coverslips
- ✓ pencil with eraser
- ✓ eyedroppers
- ✓ sewing needles
- ✓ vegetable peeler, new
- ✓ iodine
- ✓ compound microscope, with light source

Safety: Have an adult present and use care when working with biological stains. Avoid skin and eye contact. Wear safety glasses and disposable gloves. Wear disposable gloves when working with animal materials (raw meat and blood); wash your hands with soap and warm water after handling the raw meat and disposing of the gloves.

In Investigation 3 you observed that single-celled protists appear to be more complex than your cheek cell. You probably observed that some protist cells move about and/or have green chloroplasts (plastids) that allow them to make their own food. Your cheek cells neither move on their own nor have chloroplasts!

Eukaryotic cells of larger organisms—such as plants and animals—have given up their individuality to become part of a larger, more complicated multicellular organism. That is because these larger organisms are made up of tissues—groups of many cells, each with a distinct function. When an organism is multicelled, it needs its cells to be specialized: Different cells develop and function in different ways.

Let's explore some kinds of cells in multicellular organisms to learn more about cell specialization.

CELLS AND TISSUES

Tissue cells are specialized. A muscle cell, for example, has special proteins to control muscle contraction. There are different types of muscle cells. Heart and body muscle cells (called striated muscle) have proteins that form visible bands. Smooth muscles have similar proteins, but they are not organized into visible bands. Body or skeletal muscle cells allow you to move your body. Smooth muscle is found in organs such as the small and large intestine. You cannot control smooth muscle or heart muscle.

Examine various animal muscle tissues available from a butcher: beef or chicken muscle, chicken heart, natural pork casing (intestine). Place a very small piece of each in a drop of water on separate clean microscope slides. To make a teased tissue preparation, use sewing needles to separate muscle fibers in the tissue as much as possible. Add a drop of 0.1% methylene blue stain to this teased muscle tissue preparation. Add a plastic coverslip. To spread out muscle fibers as much as possible, press down on the tissue area or the coverslip with the eraser end of a pencil. You may need to add more water to fill in air bubbles. Use an eyedropper to add a drop closest to an air bubble in your preparation.

Examine each preparation under the microscope. At low magnification (40X), scan the preparation for a viewing field that shows the *edges* of teased muscle tissue. Now switch to a higher magnification (100X or 430X), and focus your attention on these tissue edges to view individual muscle cells. Compare the muscle cells in your various preparations to each of the three muscle photomicrographs in Figure 11. Can you

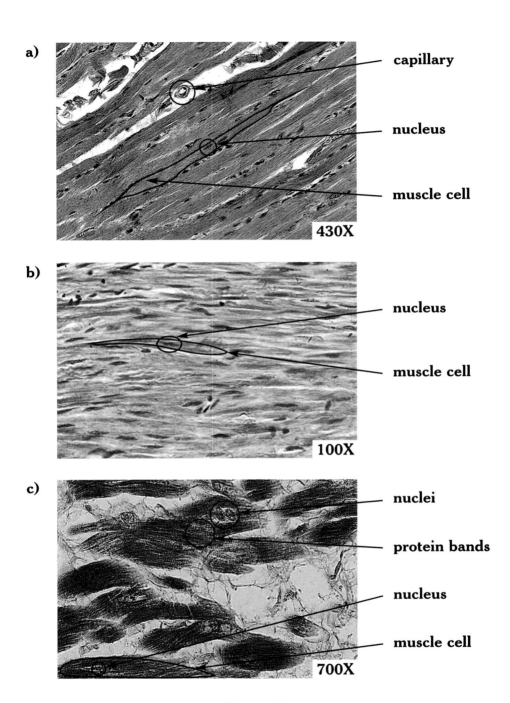

Figure 11.

a) Skeletal (striated) muscle tissue, as in chicken or beef muscle.
b) Smooth muscle tissue, as in intestine. c) Heart muscle tissue.

observe muscle protein striations? Can you identify the muscle types shown in each of these three photomicrographs?

Plants, like animals, have tissues. All plants are made up of three types of tissues: covering, support, and transport. You have already examined onion skin, a covering tissue. A plant's support tissue is found in roots, stems, and leaves. It is made up of masses of thin-walled cells. These cells support the plant and store water and food. Transport tissue, called vascular tissue, is made up of tiny tubes that carry water and nutrients throughout the plant.

Are each of these plant tissues made up of different kinds of cells? You can study cells from soft plant tissues (such as celery, broccoli, tomato, carrot, and potato) by making a section mount (see Figure 12). Start by using a new vegetable peeler to make lengthwise or cross cuts (called tissue sections) of a celery stalk. Try to peel the thinnest section possible. Add a drop of water to a clean slide. You may need to add additional drops of water (or stain) as well as a coverslip. At low magnification (40X), look for the *edges* of sectioned plant tissue. Now switch to a higher magnification (100X or 430X), and focus your attention on these tissue edges to view individual plant cells.

Use the cross section of a celery stalk in Figure 12e as a guide. The outermost layer of cells makes up the covering tissue. Below the covering tissue, and making up most of the body of the stalk and the tissue section, is support tissue.

Sectioning Soft Tissues

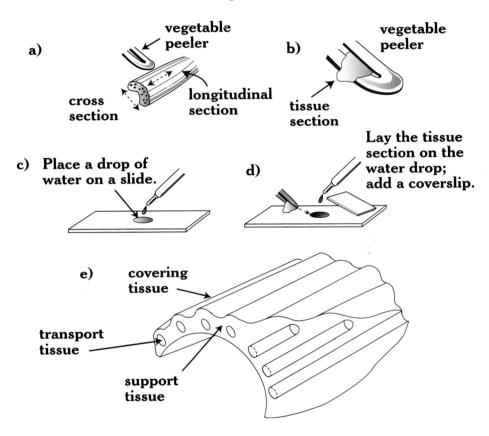

Figure 12.

MAKING A SECTION MOUNT

Sectioning soft tissues: a) Use a new vegetable peeler to make longitudinal or cross sections of plant tissue. b) Try to peel the thinnest section possible. c) Add a drop of water to a clean slide. d) You may need to add additional drops of water (or a stain) to the sample as well as a coverslip. e) Cross section of celery.

Try to find a section through a celery "string" which is actually a transport tissue. In cross section, it will look like a group of Os. Other transport tissue cells are scattered throughout the stalk support tissue. Can you see them?

Examine sections from other plant stems such as broccoli and tomato. Are their support and vascular tissue cells similar to those in celery?

You can use the iodine test to find where food is stored in a plant. Some support tissue stores starch, a plant food. Make a section mount of potato tissue and stain it with a drop of iodine. This chemical will stain starch a purplish black. Can you confirm that potato cells store starch? Make section mounts of other plant roots. Does their support tissue store starch?

Science Project Idea

Try developing tissue stains using various water-based dyes such as food coloring. Are they as effective as iodine in staining structures in cells and tissues (e.g., the cell wall)? If possible, use a computer microscope such as the QX3, or a video camera with a microscope adapter, to capture images of your preparations to illustrate your results.

Investigation 5

What Makes an Organism?

Materials

- ✓ **an adult**
- ✓ collected lichen
- ✓ razorblade, single-edged
- ✓ pencil with eraser
- ✓ eyedropper
- ✓ water
- ✓ forceps
- ✓ microscope slides
- ✓ plastic coverslips
- ✓ sewing needles
- ✓ compound microscope, with light source

An organism is any living creature—either single-celled or multicelled. Some organisms are combined organisms living closely together. When both organisms benefit, scientists call this a symbiotic relationship. One example is lichen.

To the eye, lichen appears to be a single large organism. You need a microscope to see that it is really two organisms. Lichen is a microscopic fungus and alga, or a microscopic fungus and cyanobacterium, living together. In this special association, both partners benefit. Most of the lichen body is fungus. Just under the outer fungus layer are scattered protist or cyanobacterium cells. These cells make food (sugar) through photosynthesis. Most lichens live on rocks or bark.

Ask an adult to use a single-edged razor blade to trim a *thin* slice from a lichen body. Use forceps to place this thin slice in a drop of water on a microscope slide. Use sewing needles to tease it apart. Add a plastic coverslip. To spread out the teased material as much as possible, press down on the coverslip over the tissue area with the eraser end of a pencil. You may need to add more water to push out air bubbles. Use an eyedropper to add a drop close to an air bubble in your preparation.

Use a compound microscope to observe which part is fungus (threadlike hyphae) and which is protist (colored spherical cells). Begin at low magnification (40X), then switch to a higher magnification (100X or 430X). Use Figure 13 as a guide to identifying each symbiotic partner.

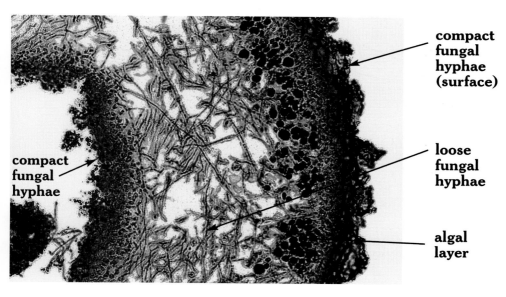

Figure 13.

MICROSCOPIC CROSS SECTION OF A LICHEN

Collect lichens and plan experiments that test whether each lichen partner is an organism. Does a green lichen partner (protist or cyanobacterium) survive if a lichen piece is placed in the dark for a month or longer? Make a wet mount of a lichen exposed to these extended dark conditions. Can you see any green photosynthetic partners? Any fungal partners? If a lichen loses its partner, can it still be called a lichen?

Scientists suspect that symbiotic relationships are more complicated than organisms living together. Are eukaryotic cells more advanced than prokaryotic cells? Why do only eukaryotic cells have organelles? Let's take a cell tour in the next chapter and find out!

Chapter 3

Cell Tours

A typical eukaryotic cell is like a miniature body containing tiny organs called organelles. Cell organelles float about in a fluid called cytoplasm. The cell's cytoplasm and organelles are contained within an envelope called the cell membrane. This membrane keeps the cell intact. It also provides channels that open and close to allow selected molecules into and out of the cell.

But why are membrane-covered organelles found only in eukaryotic cells? Today, most scientists accept the theory of endosymbiosis. This theory, first made by Lynn Margulis

(1938–   ) in the early 1970s, states that cell organelles are the descendants of prokaryotes. These prokaryotic cells entered larger cells and began a unique relationship with them 1.5 billion years ago. Examples are mitochondria and chloroplasts, two types of organelles.

In previous investigations you observed the command center of the cell—the nucleus. Other organelles provide the cell with energy. Still others manufacture proteins and additional molecules that the cell needs to survive and to communicate with the world around it. Some organelles, such as lysosomes, even digest the cell when it dies.

In this chapter you will learn to identify many cell organelles and how the organelles work together to create a functioning life unit.

Investigation 6

Is the Nucleus the Largest Organelle in a Cell?

Materials

✓ **an adult**
✓ red onion pieces
✓ *Elodea* leaf
✓ tweezers
✓ 2 eyedroppers
✓ microscope slides

✓ water
✓ coverslips
✓ iodine stain
✓ disposable gloves
✓ safety glasses
✓ compound microscope, with light source

Safety: Have an adult present and use care when working with biological stains. Avoid skin and eye contact. Wear safety glasses and disposable gloves.

British botanist Robert Brown (1773–1858) was the first to describe the nucleus during his microscopic studies of plant tissues in 1831. He pointed out that every cell had a nucleus.

You can examine nuclei in red onion skin cells. Place a drop of water in the center of a microscope slide. Use tweezers to remove the thin, transparent, skin from the thicker, fleshy part of the onion and place it in the drop of water on the slide. Add a drop of iodine stain over the onion epidermis and finish making a wet mount (see Figure 6) by adding a coverslip. Examine this preparation at low magnification (40X). You may need to reduce the lighting by using the disc or iris diaphragm. Switch to 430X magnification. The iodine stain will color certain cell structures such as the cell wall and the cell nucleus.

Can you find stained cell nuclei in onion cells? Measure the size of several onion cell nuclei. Are they all about the same size? Record your observations and measurements in your notebook. Make drawings of onion cells or photograph them using the QX3 computer microscope.

The cytoplasm of many cells, especially plant cells, contains vacuoles—spaces in the cytoplasm filled with water and dissolved materials surrounded by a single membrane. For example, the cell vacuoles of citrus fruits contain solutions of acids and other materials. Young plant cells have many vacuoles, but as they grow older they produce one central, large, fluid-filled vacuole.

Make a wet mount of an *Elodea* leaf. You can get *Elodea* at a pet or aquarium store. Use tweezers to remove a leaf from the growing tip of the plant. Make a wet mount (see Figure 6) by placing the leaf in a drop of water on a clean microscope slide. Add a coverslip and examine first at low magnification (40X), then at higher magnifications. Be sure to adjust the iris or disc diaphragm to allow enough light to pass through the leaf. Find an *Elodea* cell that contains a central vacuole and measure the cell and the vacuole. Make drawings of these vacuolated cells or photograph them using the QX3 computer microscope.

Is a cell vacuole an organelle? Is it larger or smaller than a typical plant nucleus? Can you confirm Robert Brown's observations that a plant cell's nucleus is its largest organelle?

Investigation 7

What Powers Cells?

Materials

✓ **an adult**

✓ drinking glass

✓ water

✓ drinking straw

✓ 0.1% bromothymol blue indicator

✓ watch with second hand

The life processes of cells require energy—lots of it. The production of energy by a cell is called cell respiration. In cells, energy is stored by adenosine triphosphate (ATP). The cell must constantly make ATP if it is to survive. Mitochondria are the organelles that make ATP. Some cells have thousands of mitochondria (see Figure 14). These organelles break down sugar and make the ATP molecules that the cell needs. Carbon dioxide and water are also made in this process.

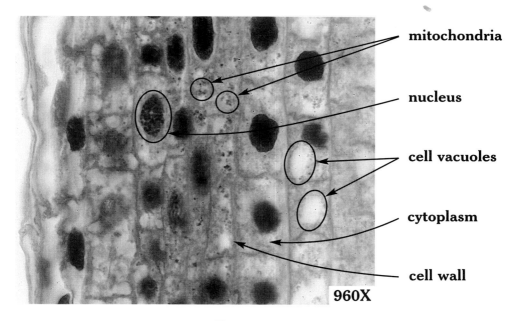

960X

Figure 14.

This highly magnified view shows groups of stained mitochondria in a section preparation of onion root-tip cells. Notice the large cell vacuoles and nuclei.

Cell Respiration

$$Food\ Molecule + O_2 \rightarrow CO_2 + H_2O + ATP$$
(Sugar)

Since mitochondria need oxygen to make ATP, they are said to participate in aerobic ("with oxygen") cellular respiration.

Do your body's cells use oxygen to produce needed energy and, at the same time, produce carbon dioxide (CO_2) gas? Ask your science teacher for bromothymol blue indicator (0.1% or less). Add a couple of drops of this indicator to half a glass of water until you observe a blue color. **Ask an adult** to place a soda straw into this colored solution and slowly blow bubbles. The exhaled carbon dioxide and water form carbonic acid [$CO_2 + H_2O \rightarrow H_2CO_3$]. This acid changes the solution's color from blue to yellow-green. Record the amount of time, in seconds, it takes the solution to return to its original blue color. **HINT:** The more CO_2 that was exhaled into the solution, the longer it will take to go back to its original blue color.

Ask the adult to begin to exercise so that certain of the body's cells (e.g., muscle cells) require more energy. After a short period of vigorous exercise, have the adult repeat bubble blowing into the blue indicator solution. Do you notice a quicker change in solution color? Record the amount of time it takes the solution to return to its original blue color. Do your exhalations, following vigorous exercise, contain more carbon dioxide gas? Does this show that your body uses oxygen to produce energy?

Investigation 8

What Separates Cells From Their Environment?

Materials

✓ **an adult**	✓ safety glasses
✓ red onion pieces	✓ disposable gloves
✓ tweezers	✓ table salt
✓ 2 eyedroppers	✓ glass of water
✓ microscope slide	✓ compound microscope, with light source
✓ coverslip	
✓ iodine stain	✓ measuring spoon

Safety: Have an adult present and use care when working with biological stains. Avoid skin and eye contact. Wear safety glasses and disposable gloves.

All living things maintain a stable internal environment, often quite different from their surroundings. The cell membrane holds the entire cell together—all its cytoplasm and organelles. It protects the cell by determining what gets in or out. Cells use their membranes to keep their internal environment stable.

Some organisms—plants, bacteria, and some protists and

fungi—also have a rigid structure outside the cell membrane called the cell wall. The cell wall provides extra support for these types of cells.

To prepare a red onion cell slide, place a drop of water in the center of a microscope slide. Use tweezers to remove the thin, transparent skin layer from the thicker, fleshy part of the onion and place it in the drop of water. Add a drop of iodine stain over the onion epidermis and finish making a wet mount (see Figure 6) by adding a coverslip. Examine this preparation at low magnification (40X). You may need to reduce the lighting by using the disc or iris diaphragm. Switch to 430X magnification. The iodine stain will color certain cell structures such as the cell membrane and cell wall.

You can use a salt solution to pull the cell membrane away from the cell wall. Then you can see the cell wall more easily when you stain it with iodine. To do this, add 2 tablespoons of table salt to a glass of water to create a concentrated salt solution. Make a new wet mount of red onion epidermis. Use a drop or two of the salt water instead of water, to make the wet mount of onion cells. Add a drop of iodine stain as before. Observe the preparation at 100X magnification.

What happens to the cytoplasm inside the cells? Can you observe the cell wall more easily? Can you see the cell membrane? How does your preparation compare with the cells shown in Figure 15?

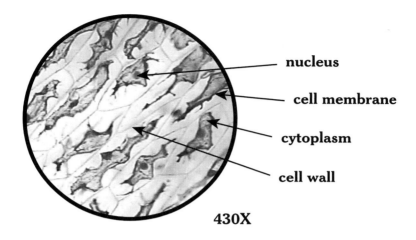

nucleus

cell membrane

cytoplasm

cell wall

430X

Figure 15.

Flooding onion tissue with salt water causes water in the cell to move outside the cell. This water movement shrinks the cell so that the cell membrane can be easily observed. What cell process does this water movement illustrate?

Chapter 4

Cell Processes

All cells must maintain a stable internal environment to obtain energy, perform their specific assignments, grow, and in many cases move about and reproduce.

Cells show us metabolism—chemical reactions and physical processes that maintain life functions. No object less complex than a cell can support itself.

In this chapter you will take a closer look at the many facets of cell metabolism, growth, movement, and reproduction.

Investigation 9

What Keeps Plants Stiff?

Materials

- ✓ measuring spoons
- ✓ salt
- ✓ 2 drinking glasses
- ✓ red onion
- ✓ eyedropper
- ✓ paper towels
- ✓ bottled water
- ✓ scissors
- ✓ ruler
- ✓ celery stalks
- ✓ microscope slides
- ✓ coverslips
- ✓ clothespin
- ✓ compound microscope, with light source

A solution is a mixture of different types of molecules in a liquid. One type of molecule is the solvent, or the substance in which the other substance is dissolved. In living cells, the solvent is water. The substance that is dissolved in the solvent is called the solute. An example of a solute is salt.

Many kinds of molecules move into and out of cells. The most important is water. The cell membrane acts as a barrier to certain types of molecules, but not water. The movement of water molecules through a membrane is a process called osmosis. In general, water movement in osmosis will be from a region of lower solute concentration to a region of higher solute concentration.

Plant cells contain greater amounts of solutes than the outside environment. As a result, water tends to move into plant cells. This movement of water creates pressure (called turgor) within the cell against the cell wall.

What happens if turgor is lost in a plant cell? Since fewer solutes in a solution outside a plant cell keep up turgor, what happens if more solutes are added to the solution outside the plant cell?

Add 2 teaspoons of salt to a glass of water to create a concentrated salt solution. Make a wet mount of red onion skin (see Figure 6). Cut or tear a number of triangle-shaped pieces of paper towel.

Use an eyedropper to place a drop(s) of salt solution on one side of the coverslip so that it just mixes with the existing fluid of the wet mount. Carefully insert one point of the triangular piece of paper towel underneath the opposite side of the coverslip. Use Figure 16 as a guide. Observe this preparation at 100X magnification. You may need to reduce the lighting by using the disc or iris diaphragm. What happens to the cytoplasm inside cells exposed to this concentrated salt solution? Can you reverse these changes? Try doing so by adding drops of bottled water to flush out the excess salt solution and inserting another triangular piece of paper towel on the opposite side.

Design an experiment that explores wilting—water loss from plant cells. Pour bottled water into two glasses, filling them halfway. To one glass add 3 tablespoons of salt. Stir to dissolve the salt. Measure and cut two fresh celery stalks to equal lengths of about 8 inches. Immerse one stalk in the glass of water and the other stalk in the glass of salt water. Record in your notebook what happens over the next hour or two. Does one celery stalk's cells lose water (e.g., wilt), while the other does not?

Based upon your investigations of water movement in cells, what would you recommend florists do to prevent wilting?

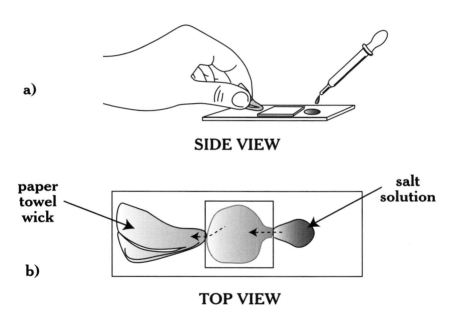

Figure 16.

MOVING SOLUTIONS

a) Place a drop of salt water on one side of the wet mount and a piece of paper towel on the other side. b) The paper towel "wick" will pull salt solution under the coverslip. What happens when the cells are exposed to the salt solution?

Science Project Idea

Investigate the role of sugar on potato cells. Use an apple corer to make 3 potato cores that are identical in size. A suggested size would be a 3-inch length. Obtain an electronic scale balance. Number and weigh each potato core. Record these weights in your notebook. Prepare a concentrated sugar solution by adding 1 cup of granulated sugar (sucrose) to 1 pint of bottled water. Stir until all the sugar has dissolved. Label the solution SOLUTION #1—HIGH SUGAR SOLUTION. Also prepare a dilute sugar solution by mixing 1 cup of the concentrated sugar solution with 1 cup bottled water. Label this solution SOLUTION #2—LOW SUGAR SOLUTION. Label a third container BOTTLED WATER and fill it with bottled water.

Now immerse one potato core each into the two sugar solutions and the plain bottled water. Wait 20 to 30 minutes. Remove each core and carefully blot excess moisture from it with a paper towel. Carefully weigh each of the cores on the balance and record their weights in your notebook. Which potato core gained the most weight? Which lost weight? Which neither gained nor lost weight? Based on your experimental data, which solution, salt or sugar, would be best used in keeping plants from wilting?

Investigation 10

How Do Cells Eat and Move?

Materials

- ✓ **an adult**
- ✓ teaspoon
- ✓ bottled water
- ✓ small paper cup
- ✓ eyedropper
- ✓ 0.1% methylene blue stain
- ✓ safety glasses
- ✓ disposable gloves
- ✓ 1 packet active dry yeast
- ✓ toothpicks
- ✓ amoebas (from science supply company)
- ✓ microscope slides

- ✓ coverslips
- ✓ grass clippings
- ✓ canning jar with lid
- ✓ polyethylene oxide
- ✓ liquid measuring cup
- ✓ small plastic cup
- ✓ wooden craft stick
- ✓ *Elodea* leaves
- ✓ watch with second hand
- ✓ flashlight
- ✓ compound microscope, with light source
- ✓ tweezers

Safety: Have an adult present and use care when working with biological stains. Avoid skin and eye contact. Wear safety glasses and disposable gloves.

In Investigation 9 you learned how cells move water across their cell membrane to balance the concentration of dissolved salts. But how do cells take in very large particles? They bring large particles inside themselves by a process known as cell eating, or phagocytosis.

OBSERVING HOW CELLS EAT

White blood cells use phagocytosis to protect the body from infection. They search for and eat bacteria. Phagocytosis is also common among certain single-celled protists like *Amoeba*. Let's investigate cell eating in *Amoeba*.

Amoebas are single-celled protists that are hard to collect or observe in nature. They may be obtained from science supply companies (see Appendix C).

Add a teaspoon of bottled water to a small paper cup. Add 2 to 5 drops of 0.1% methylene blue stain to color the water a very deep blue. Add pinches of active dry yeast to the colored water in the paper cup. Mix the yeast into the colored water to make a colored paste. Obtain some colored yeast cells by dipping the end of a toothpick into the paste. Transfer the colored yeast cells to a drop of water on a clean microscope slide containing amoebas. Complete the wet mount preparation by adding a coverslip (see Figure 6).

Examine the slide first at low magnification (40X) to locate an amoeba. Be sure to adjust the iris or disc diaphragm to not allow too much light to pass through the sample. Once you have located an amoeba, switch to a higher magnification (100X or 430X). Carefully focus on a single amoeba cell. Observe the amoeba. How does it move? How does it take in food? Does it eat the colored yeast cells? Record your observations in your notebook. You might want to make a small movie clip of this process using a QX3 computer microscope.

HOW SOME CELLS MOVE ABOUT

Ciliates are protists that move about using hairlike structures called cilia (see Appendix A). You can obtain ciliates from almost any collected water sample or from a grass infusion. An infusion is a special water solution used to grow certain microbes. Make a grass infusion by placing some chopped grass clippings or timothy hay in the bottom of a canning jar. Add collected or bottled water. Place a lid loosely on top of the jar. Let it stand in indirect light. The sill of a north-facing window is an excellent location. Use an eyedropper to sample your infusion. Infusions can be sources of microbes for weeks or months.

You will need to add a barrier that will slow infusion microlife down without harming them. The protist-slowing solution will enable you to view cell movement and internal cell functions more easily. Make the slowing solution by thoroughly mixing 1 teaspoon of polyethylene oxide (Appendix C) in 3 ounces (90 mL) of warm water in a small plastic cup. Stir the mixture continually with a wooden craft stick to make sure all the polyethylene oxide goes into solution.

Use an eyedropper to sample the scum layer in a prepared grass infusion. There you will almost certainly find *Paramecium*, a single-celled ciliate. Use Figure 17a to confirm that you have *Paramecium*.

To observe *Paramecium* feeding, make a wet mount (see Figure 6) by mixing a drop of infusion water with a drop of protist-slowing solution on a clean microscope slide. Mix the two drops with a toothpick. Add a drop of colored yeast cells as before. Mix the drops and add a coverslip. Examine the preparation under the microscope.

Examine first at low magnification (40X) to locate a paramecium. Be sure to adjust the iris or disc diaphragm to not allow too much light to pass through the infusion sample. Once you have located a single *Paramecium* that seems to be standing still, switch to a higher magnification (100X or 430X). The protist-slowing solution is providing a physical barrier to the cell, allowing you to observe its beating cilia. Cilia are short, hairlike structures that usually occur in groups on the surface of the ciliate. Each cilium can be compared to an arm of a swimmer. The beating action propels the cell through the water. Some ciliates, like *Paramecium*, have their entire bodies covered by cilia (see Figure 17a). These cilia beat in waves. Can you observe this? Keep scanning the paramecium cell. Can you also observe the colored yeast particles being taken into the cell through a structure called the oral groove? Closely monitor the colored yeast cells. What happens to them over time?

No doubt you will also observe other single cells, each having long hairlike structures called complex flagella. Flagella are like cilia, except longer. Cells that have flagella are called

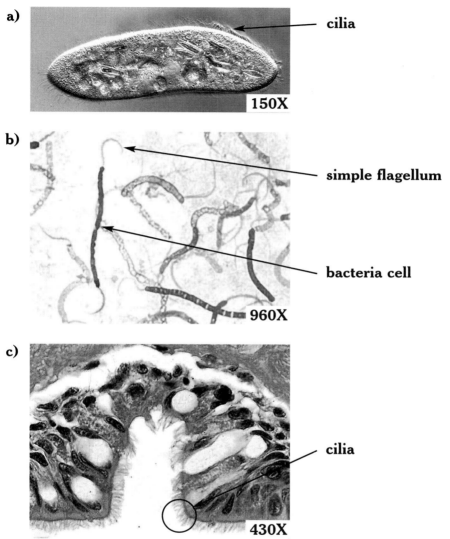

Figure 17.

a) The protist *Paramecium* is covered in cilia. b) Some bacteria cells (e.g., *Bacillus subtilis*) have simple flagella that move them through an inner-space world. c) Special ciliated cells line the human trachea to move dirt and dust particles toward the mouth to be expelled.

flagellates (see Figure 17b). Although most of these cells are smaller than ciliates, they are plentiful in grass infusions. Use the section of the table on page 121 ("The Microbe Identification Guide") to identify as many as you can. Do flagellates swim as fast as ciliates?

Other eukaryote cells also have cilia. Look at the tissue section of the upper human respiratory tract in Figure 17c. Can you identify ciliated epithelial cells? These ciliated "lining" cells help remove particles and material that pass into the airway. These cells are some of the first to be destroyed by cigarette smoke.

CYTOPLASMIC STREAMING

Another discovery Robert Brown made with his single-lens microscope was the circulation of cytoplasm (cell fluid) and the cell structures (organelles) such as chloroplasts in the fluid. This circulation is called cytoplasmic streaming or cyclosis. A good subject for observing cell cyclosis is the aquarium plant *Elodea*. Obtain *Elodea* at a pet or aquarium store. Use tweezers to remove a leaf from the growing tip of the plant. Make a wet mount (see Figure 6) by placing the leaf in a drop of water on a clean microscope slide. Add a coverslip and examine first at low magnification (40X), then at higher magnifications. Be sure to adjust the iris or disc diaphragm to allow enough light to pass through the leaf. Carefully focus on a single *Elodea* cell. Compare your field of view with Figure 10b. Can you see small, green, oval-shaped chloroplasts inside an *Elodea* cell? How large are they?

Use the second hand of a watch (or a stopwatch) to time the movement of these cell organelles. How long does it take a chloroplast to make a trip around the interior of the plant cell?

Can you calculate just how fast chloroplasts move inside an *Elodea* cell? Use the measurement skills you learned in Investigation 1 to measure the length of an *Elodea* cell. To obtain the rate of their movement, divide the length of the cell (in micrometers) by the time (in seconds) it takes a chloroplast to travel that distance. Do chloroplasts travel faster inside a cell exposed to a lot of light (light from a flashlight shined on the slide preparation) or much lower light conditions? Does cytoplasmic streaming in *Elodea* cells always occur in the same direction?

Science Project Ideas

● Design an experiment that compares cytoplasmic streaming in a protist, like *Amoeba*, to that in a plant cell, like *Elodea*.

● Investigate how fast a ciliate or flagellate travels in a pondwater sample.

Investigation 11

How Quickly Do Cells Reproduce?

Materials

- ✓ Figure 18
- ✓ Table 5
- ✓ calculator

All organisms need to reproduce. During cell division, cellular material is divided between two new cells. In one-celled organisms, cell division increases the number of individuals in a population: Each cell makes a new cell (or organism). In multicellular organisms, the result of cell division is growth. At first, a cell grows by taking in food. The cell uses nutrients to make organelles such as chloroplasts and mitochondria. In Investigation 1 you learned that a cell cannot keep on growing. At some point it gets so large that it cannot continue to carry out its functions—so it must divide.

Prokaryotic cells reproduce by dividing in two. They have one simple circular chromosome. Before dividing, the chromosome is duplicated, with one copy going to each of two new daughter cells.

Eukaryotic cells reproduce through a more complicated process called the cell cycle. The cell cycle includes three phases: interphase, mitosis, and cytokinesis. During interphase, the cell grows. Toward the end of interphase, DNA is copied. Then the cell begins to divide—the phase known as mitosis. During mitosis, the duplicated DNA (in complex chromosomes) is divided equally into two daughter nuclei. Finally, the daughter cells' cytoplasm separates in a process called cytokinesis. Use Table 5 as a guide to each phase and step in the cell cycle in onion cells.

Onion or garlic root tips are good plant parts for studying the cell cycle. Roots have various regions, as shown in Figure 18a. The root cap provides protection to the tender root tip as it grows through the soil. Just behind the root cap is an area called the region of cell elongation. This region contains the highest percentage of cells undergoing cell division. As the cells divide in this region, the root tip lengthens, pushing itself farther into the soil.

Onion root tip cells take about 24 hours (1,440 minutes) for one complete cell cycle. Other eukaryotic cells, such as the protist *Paramecium*, take only hours to divide. Certain bacterial cells may divide every six minutes. Some cells in our bodies, such as liver cells, normally divide very slowly. But if a portion of the liver is removed (e.g., in a liver transplant), liver cells will begin to copy themselves until the liver reaches its former size. (This is a process called regeneration.) All told, about 2 trillion cell divisions occur in your body every 24 hours!

How much time does an onion root tip cell spend in each phase of the cell cycle? Figure 18b contains magnified views

Table 5.

THE CELL CYCLE OF AN ONION

Phase	Step	Description	Image
Interphase	Interphase	The longest phase of the cell cycle, it includes growth, production of proteins and other cell products, and duplication of DNA.	
M I T O S I S	Prophase	Normally dispersed genetic material, chromatin, begins to condense into visible chromosomes. The spindle apparatus begins to form. The spindle will act as a guide for the movement of the chromosomes.	
	Metaphase	Chromosomes have been completely condensed and copied. These DNA copies are called sister chromatids, joined together at the center by the centromere. The chromatids, attached to spindle fibers, line up at the center of the cell at an area called the equator.	
	Anaphase	Sister chromatids separate at the centromere and begin to be pulled to opposite sides of the cell by the spindle fibers.	
	Telophase	The two sets of chromosomes that are now separated and are at each end of the cell. Two new nuclear membranes begin to form around the separate sets of chromosomes, and the DNA begins to disperse into the chromatin again. A cleavage furrow (in animal cells) or the cell plate (in plant cells) begins to form.	
Cytokinesis	Cytokinesis	Cytoplasm divides.	

a)

b)

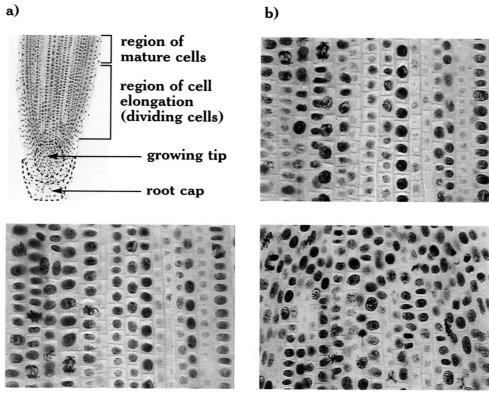

- region of mature cells
- region of cell elongation (dividing cells)
- growing tip
- root cap

Figure 18.

a) The regions of a root tip. b) MITOSIS. Determine the cell cycle phase of the cells in each of these three images.

of actively dividing root tip cells. Use Table 5 as a guide in determining the cell cycle phase for each cell in the photomicrograph. For example, if 10 out of 100 cells in the photomicrograph were found to be in prophase, the percentage of cells in this mitotic stage is 10/100 = 10%. Therefore, if any one cell spends 10 percent of the time in prophase, it spends $0.10 \times 1{,}440$ minutes, or 144 minutes (2 hours, 24 minutes) in this stage.

Record your calculated cell cycle times in your notebook. Compare your data to the author's data, listed below.

AUTHOR'S DATA

- 82 interphase cells counted (19 hr., 41 min.)

- 9 prophase cells counted (2 hr., 9 min.)

- 4 metaphase cells counted (58 min.)

- 3 anaphase cells counted (43 min.)

- 2 telophase cells counted (29 min.)

Chapter 5

Microbes You Know as Bacteria

Bacteria are invisible to the naked eye except in large concentrations (called colonies). They can be found in every environment on, in, and above the earth: in soil and ocean sediments; in the air; in and on plants and animals from fleas to elephants; and in and on humans. Bacteria live on our skin, in our mouths, and in our intestines.

We tend to think that bacteria are only harmful, causing disease, discomfort, and sometimes death. Although some bacteria do cause all these things, most bacteria are helpful. For example, bacteria keep our skin clean and help us digest our food.

On a larger scale, bacteria are necessary for life to continue on earth. Bacteria are important in the cycling of food and wastes through ecosystems. How do bacteria do this? The number of environments (microhabitats) available to bacteria (and other microbes such as fungi and protists) is greater than those available to plants and animals. Bacteria can live in these habitats because of their small size and their ability to reproduce very fast. Bacteria process or release the major gases in our atmosphere (oxygen, nitrogen, and hydrogen), and feed on organic wastes and the remains of dead organisms. In this manner, bacteria are the major recyclers of the chemical components of life.

Investigation 12

How Do Bacteria Populations Interact?

Materials

✓ 2 clear plastic 1-liter soda bottles

✓ tin snips

✓ shredded paper (a piece of newsprint about 4 in × 4 in, or 10 cm × 10 cm)

✓ hard-boiled egg yolk (sulfur source)

✓ marsh or pond muds, or gutter muds

✓ sand

✓ collected water (marsh, pond, gutter)

✓ plastic wrap

✓ rubber band

✓ aluminum foil or black construction paper

✓ colored pencils

✓ measuring spoon

✓ small amounts of any of the following:

+ dried grass or leaves

+ straw

+ bits of bark

+ small pieces of metal

+ dried manure (horse, cow) from a garden center

+ seashells

+ soap

+ pine needles

+ table salt

+ Epsom salts (sulfate source)

You can establish a microbial garden in a Winogradsky column. This column will allow you to view the effect of different environmental conditions on bacteria. The Winogradsky column you will make is based on a more elaborate one made by Russian microbiologist Sergei Winogradsky (1856–1953).

Carefully remove the necks of two clear plastic 1-liter soda bottles using tin snips. The bottles will become Winogradsky columns. You will make two of them so that you can investigate the effects of various environmental conditions on bacteria populations.

Use Figure 19 as a guide in making your column(s). Mix sand or collected mud with 1 tablespoon (15 mL) of hard-boiled egg yolk. Add some shredded paper. Mix well. Layer sand and mud in the column. You may choose to add and mix other materials listed in the materials list. Pour water from the collection source (marsh, puddle, swamp) over the sand-mud mixture until there is a small amount of unabsorbed water on top. Cover the column with plastic wrap, secured by a rubber band.

In your notebook, make a detailed diagram showing the placement of all materials added to the column. These notes will come in handy later, helping you understand how the materials affect developing microhabitats.

Put the columns in places with different environmental conditions: light-exposed or dark (covered with aluminum foil or black paper), warm or cool, tightened lid or lidless. For example, a rich culture of photosynthetic bacteria will develop in a couple of weeks in a column left in sunlight. A similar column kept in the dark will not have photosynthetic bacteria.

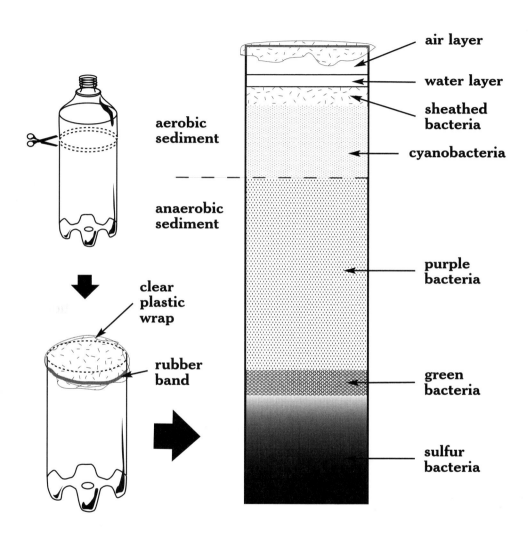

Figure 19.

BACTERIAL POPULATIONS

**The Winogradsky column allows you to culture many
bacteria populations at the same time.**

Observe the changes you see taking place over a period of several months. Record observations every one to two weeks in your notebook. Use colored pencils to illustrate the color patterns you see. Colored zones in your Winogradsky column will indicate various bacterial populations. Use Figure 19 as a guide in identifying various microbe communities. Do certain areas change color over time? Do you think that this is a visible sign of a changing bacterial population? Do certain bacteria populations seem to grow close to one another? Do other bacteria populations always seem to grow apart?

Science Project Idea

Obtain a long, thin plastic straw (e.g., coffee-stirring stick). Use it as a micro-sampler to obtain samples of growing bacteria populations inside your column. Place your index finger over the top hole of the straw and carefully insert the sampling tube down into the mud and ooze. Once you reach an area of interest, remove your index finger to draw bacteria into the tube. Replace your finger on the tube and remove it from the column. Allow several drops of collected material to fall in the center of a clean microscope slide. Use a flat-ended toothpick to spread the drops into a film that you allow to dry. Stain the film with 0.1% crystal violet stain (see Figure 8).

Determine if these sampled microhabitats are acidic or basic. Place a drop of a collected sample on a piece of litmus or pH paper. Record the results of these tests in your notebook. Are there certain layers in the Winogradsky column that are more acidic than others? Do you think these microhabitat conditions relate to the materials placed in the column?

If possible, use a camera to take close-up pictures of your column, from various angles of view, as a photographic record of bacteria populations over time. See Appendix B to learn more about image processing.

Investigation 13

How Effective Is Pasteurization?

Materials

✓ **an adult**

✓ 2 pint or quart cartons of milk, freshly purchased

✓ electronic thermometer

✓ refrigerator

✓ 2 paper cups

✓ permanent marker, fine point

✓ metric ruler

✓ 0.1% methylene blue stain

✓ safety glasses

✓ disposable gloves

✓ cotton swab

✓ microscope slides

✓ coverslips

✓ clothespin

✓ compound microscope, with light source

Safety: Have an adult present and use care when working with biological stains. Avoid skin and eye contact. Wear safety glasses and disposable gloves.

Until around 1860, the existence of bacteria and how they worked was not known. The first breakthrough came when French microbiologist Louis Pasteur (1822–1895) was able to show the harmful effect of the growth of some microbes in wine and later in milk. He introduced a heating method that killed certain harmful bacteria. Twenty years later the dairy industry began to investigate Pasteur's process, now called pasteurization. Pasteurization uses heat to slow milk spoilage caused by microbes. It also eliminates microbes that cause disease.

Commercially, pasteurization can be performed two ways—by slow or fast exposure to heat. The slow process involves placing milk in large vats and heating it to a temperature of 145°F (63°C) for 30 minutes. The fast process involves exposing milk to a temperature of 161°F (72°C) for a brief, 15-second period. Most foods are pasteurized using the fast process. Pasteurization temperatures are not high enough to change the taste of milk. But they *are* sufficient to control the presence of disease-causing (pathogenic) bacteria. Until pasteurization, the tuberculosis bacterium, *Mycobacterium tuberculosis*, was the most heat-resistant microbe associated with milk-borne infections.

Let's investigate how many microbes survive in milk after pasteurization.

You will be counting the number of bacteria in a pasteurized milk sample. Use a permanent marker and a metric ruler to draw a 1-cm square in the middle of a glass microscope slide. This area will hold about 0.01 mL of milk evenly spread over the slide.

Obtain two freshly purchased pint or quart cartons of milk, both having the same expiration date. In your notebook, record the date the containers of milk were purchased and the expiration date. Use an electronic thermometer to measure the temperature in your home refrigerator. Record this data in your notebook.

Open one carton and carefully pour a very small amount of milk into a paper cup. Close the carton and place it, along with the unopened carton, in the refrigerator.

Dip a cotton swab into the small cup of milk. Squeeze any excess milk from the swab by pressing it against the side of the cup. Carefully rub the milk sample over the slide containing the centimeter square. Make sure that the sample covers the entire area of the square. Allow the sample to air dry. Now you can stain the smear, using Figure 8 as a guide. Flood the centimeter square with 0.1% methylene blue stain. Allow it to sit for 1 minute. Use a water-filled eyedropper to wash (one drop at a time) the stain off the slide into a paper cup. Allow the stained preparation to dry. View the preparation under high magnification (430X or higher). Count the number of bacteria cells present in a field of view. Since this is not a raw (unpasteurized) milk sample, do not expect to observe many bacteria cells. Record your count in your notebook. Now, move to another new viewing field within the centimeter square. Again, count the number of bacteria cells observed within the field of view. Obtain counting data for at least 10 viewing fields. Average the counts by dividing the total number of cells counted by the number of fields observed. Multiply this number by either of the following factors:

200,000 if a 43X objective was used (430X total magnification)
500,000 if a 96X objective was used (960X total magnification)

For example, say you count an average of 9 bacteria cells in each of the 10 viewing fields at 430X magnification. The estimated number of bacteria in 1 liter of milk would be:

$$9 \times 200,000 = 1,800,000 \text{ cells per liter, or } 1,800 \text{ cells per milliliter}$$

Currently, most state and federal health regulations require a bacteria count of no higher than 2.5 million cells per liter, or 25,000 cells per milliliter.

Does your milk sample meet established health standards? At the expiration date, prepare stained smears of both the unopened and the opened carton of milk. Are bacteria counts below health standards? How long, at refrigeration temperatures, will an opened carton of milk last beyond the printed expiration date—that is, does the sample continue to meet the federal health regulation standard?

Science Project Idea

Devise an experiment that determines how long an opened carton of milk can be left at room temperature before established health standards are exceeded. Make stained smear preparations (see Figure 8) of this warmed milk sample at half-hour intervals. What types of bacteria (rods, spheres, or spirals) do you observe over the exposure period?

Chapter **6**

Microbes You Know as Fungi

Almost everyone is familiar with mushrooms. They are the large, visible, fruiting bodies of fungi. One individual fungus in Oregon, the honey mushroom, covers 2,200 acres and may be thousands of years old.

There are many more, smaller types of fungi—visible only with either a magnifying glass or a microscope. These microbes are collectively called microfungi—molds, mildews, yeasts, and rusts.

Fungi are the earth's scavengers. Along with bacteria, they perform an invaluable service. Fungi make nutrients from dead plants and animals available to other cells and organisms. They do this by secreting digestive enzymes to break down nutrients. Fungi are capable of digesting almost anything, as long as the food is in a moist environment.

Many microfungi cause diseases, especially in plants. Gardeners and farmers constantly battle against molds, mildews, and rusts that attack plants. Many other microfungi form mutual relationships with plants: They help provide recycled nutrients to their root systems. Others, like yeasts, are used in making breads and alcoholic beverages. Some are used in industrial chemicals and medicines.

Investigation 14

How Do Molds Grow?

Materials

✓ **an adult**
✓ plastic container with lid
✓ bread with no preservatives
✓ teaspoon
✓ water
✓ cotton swab
✓ screwdriver
✓ magnifying glass
✓ metric ruler

✓ toothpick
✓ 0.1% methylene blue stain
✓ safety glasses
✓ disposable gloves
✓ microscope slides
✓ coverslips
✓ clothespin
✓ eyedropper
✓ compound microscope, with light source

Safety: Have an adult present and use care when working with biological stains. Avoid skin and eye contact. Wear safety glasses and disposable gloves.

Molds and other microfungi reproduce by releasing cells called spores. When spores land on a new surface, they germinate and grow slender tubes called hyphae. A single mold can produce more than a mile's worth of hyphae in just four hours.

Before the next generation of molds can reproduce, fruiting bodies must grow up from the hyphae. A fruiting body has a spore case (sporangium) that contains spores. The spore case usually sits on top of a slender stalk (see Figure 20a).

Most molds require high humidity for growth. In this investigation you will build a moisture chamber to grow collected molds. Slices of bread (those made without preservatives) will be your mold food. Your task is to learn how a mold uses its food to grow.

Begin your mold studies by placing a slice of bread on the inside lid of a margarine or frozen whipped topping container. Sprinkle 1 or 2 teaspoons (5 or 10 mL) of water on the bread. Use a cotton swab to pick up fungal spores from various sources: tree trunks, the soil surface in a flower pot or garden, plant leaves, etc. Lightly swab the cotton applicator over the surface of bread to inoculate it (transfer fungal spores to it). With a screwdriver, punch several holes in the bottom of the container and place the container upside-down on the lid.

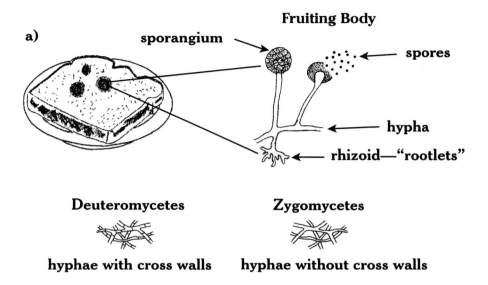

a)

sporangium

Fruiting Body

spores

hypha

rhizoid—"rootlets"

Deuteromycetes

hyphae with cross walls

Zygomycetes

hyphae without cross walls

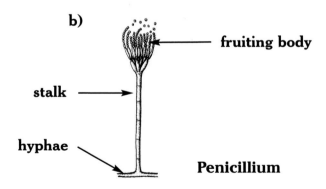

b)

stalk

hyphae

fruiting body

Penicillium

Figure 20.

a) The fruiting body of a mold makes spores. When spores germinate on a surface, they make hyphae. Deuteromycete molds have cross walls on their hyphae; zygomycetes do not. b) This illustration of *Penicillium* shows fruiting body and hypha.

Open the container daily and use a magnifying glass to observe the bread's surface for fungal hyphae. In your notebook, describe what you see happening. How long does it take for a growing mold to make fruiting bodies? How do molds grow: in a specific direction, or everywhere? Use a ruler to measure how fast a mold grows in a day.

You can use a moisture chamber and bread growth medium to see how many types of molds you can collect and look at. Under the microscope, the hyphae of some molds (a group called the deuteromycetes) have tiny structures called cross walls. Other mold hyphae (a group called the zygomycetes) do not have cross walls (see Figure 20a). Use a clean toothpick to mix a sample of hyphae (cottony material) into a drop of 0.1% methylene blue stain (or bottled water) on a microscope slide. Add a coverslip. Refer to Figure 8 to guide you in staining fungal hyphae.

Examine the preparation first at low magnification (40X), then at higher magnifications. Be sure to adjust the iris or disc diaphragm to not allow too much light to pass through the sample. Use "The Microbe Identification Guide" (Appendix A) to help you identify the different molds you see.

Science Project Ideas

● Design an experiment to see what temperatures are best for mold growth. At what temperatures do molds start and stop growing?

● Investigate the effectiveness of certain commercial preservatives (e.g., calcium propionate, sodium benzoate, and others found on ingredient lists on bread packages) on mold growth in bread products. Make sure you use two different samples of bread: one baked without preservatives and one baked with preservatives (check the ingredient lists). Make a table that compares the molding time of breads with various commercial preservatives.

● Explore your refrigerator, bread box, or other food storage areas for signs of microfungi. Do different molds grow on different foods? Make a stained smear of observed molds. Can you classify them? Make drawings of your microscopic observations in your notebook. Are they similar to the ones in "The Microbe Identification Guide" (Appendix A)?

Investigation 15

How Does a Certain Microbe Cause a Certain Disease?

Materials

✓ **an adult**

✓ fresh oranges or nectarines

✓ moldy orange

✓ potato dextrose agar culture plates (from science teacher)

✓ box of toothpicks (pointed end)

✓ box of toothpicks (flat-ended)

✓ transparent sticky tape

✓ microscope slide

✓ 0.1% methylene blue stain or 0.1% crystal violet stain

✓ safety glasses

✓ disposable gloves

✓ eyedropper

✓ magnifying glass

✓ paper punch

✓ 1-in × 3-in white index card

✓ clear tape

✓ compound microscope

Safety: Have an adult present and use care when working with biological stains. Avoid skin and eye contact. Wear safety glasses and disposable gloves.

Germs are microbes (bacteria, protists, or fungi) that are capable of growing at the expense of another organism. Some germs are pathogens—they cause a disease.

Robert Koch (1843–1910) was a German microbiologist.

He was trying to find out whether a microbe, obtained from a diseased patient, was in fact the cause of the disease. This led him to formulate Koch's postulates—a set of conditions that need to be met to verify whether a particular germ is the cause of a particular disease.

Can you demonstrate whether *Penicillium notatum* is the fungus that causes moldy orange disease? To do so, according to Koch's postulates, you must be able to do the following:

1. Describe and record the symptoms. The germ should be present only on diseased specimens and not on healthy ones.

2. Isolate the suspected pathogen from the infected plant material and establish a pure culture.

3. Use the pure culture to infect new, healthy plant material. Describe and record the symptoms shown by the new plant. Check that these are the same as recorded earlier.

4. Re-isolate the organism. Check that it is the same one as was isolated previously.

Molds grow best on a commercial culture plate medium called potato dextrose agar. You can obtain culture plates from your science teacher or through one of the sources in Appendix C.

Obtain a moldy orange. You might try leaving an orange on your counter for a few weeks. You can also ask the produce manager at your supermarket if he has one. If you tell him it is for a science project, he may be happy to give you an orange with mold on it.

You can test Koch's postulates in moldy fruit disease. In your notebook, describe what you observe in the moldy orange. If possible, use a camera to take a picture of moldy fruit disease.

To make a press mount preparation of moldy orange tissue, add a drop of 0.1% methylene blue or 0.1% crystal violet stain to the center of a clean microscope slide. Cut off a 2- to 3-inch piece of sticky tape and fold each end in on itself to create two small flaps. Now hold the tape piece by its flaps and gently touch the middle of the sticky surface to the diseased (moldy) area of the orange. A small amount of diseased tissue will adhere to the sticky surface. Now carefully press the sticky tape onto the microscope slide. Make sure that the moldy tissue contacts the stain drop.

Look at your slide under a compound microscope, first at low magnification (100X), then at high magnification (430X). Can you identify a particular microbe such as *Penicillium*—the known pathogen in moldy fruit disease? Remember, as the plant becomes weak, several types of scavenging microbes often invade. Confirm that the blue-green mold is *Penicillium*. (Compare your samples to the *Penicillium* pictures in Figure 21.) If not, search for another fruit that is infected with *Penicillium*.

Next, you want to establish a pure *Penicillium* culture—the culture in which the only microbe growing is *Penicillium*.

a)

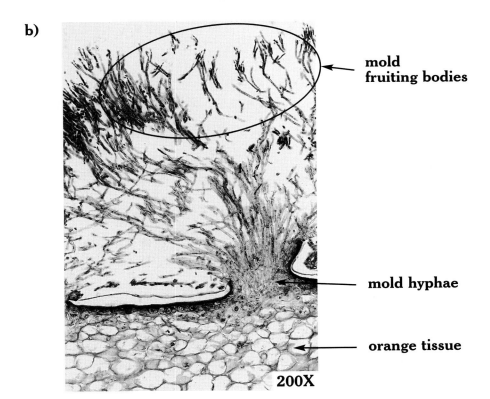

b)

mold
fruiting bodies

mold hyphae

orange tissue

Figure 21.

a) *Penicillium* colony. The light outer area is the actively
growing part of the colony. The center is a solid mass of crusty
hyphae. b) A section through an orange showing growing
Penicillium (moldy fruit disease).

You will be using a sterile flat-ended toothpick to transfer *Penicillium* from the orange to the culture plate. An unopened box of toothpicks contains sterile pieces. Carefully open a small hole in the corner of a box; gently shake the box to obtain a toothpick. Use a toothpick to scoop out as much of the diseased orange tissue containing the mold as possible. Remember, you do not want to touch the culture plate surface, or inside plate surfaces, with anything but the material you are transferring. If you do, you may transfer unwanted microbes. Raise the cover of a potato dextrose agar culture plate and deposit the diseased orange tissue in the center of it. Replace the culture plate lid and incubate the plate at room temperature for several days. Observe the closed culture plate for signs of *Penicillium* growth daily.

Use another sterile flat-ended toothpick to obtain a small sample of the growing mold after three to five days. **Be careful not to touch the toothpick to any other surface other than where the mold is growing.** Transfer some of the mold to the sticky surface of a piece of tape. Make a press mount preparation by placing the tape with mold culture, sticky surface down, on top of a drop of 0.1% methylene blue on a microscope slide. Examine this preparation under low magnification (100X), then a higher magnification (430X) of a compound microscope. Have you achieved a pure culture of *Penicillium?*

Fruits and other plant tissues usually become infected by mold following a bruise or a wound. To infect healthy plant tissues with your pure culture, use a clean pointed-tip toothpick to create a small puncture in the skin of a fresh orange or nectarine. Use another sterile, pointed toothpick to gather bits of mold from the pure culture plate. Carefully rub this mold into the punctured area of the fruit. Place the fruit in a warm place. Observe it carefully using a magnifying glass for seven to ten days. Record your observations in your notebook. Do your observations of the fruit's symptoms agree with your earlier ones?

Now, try to re-isolate the organism from this new piece of fruit in pure culture as you did before. Are you able to grow the mold in pure culture? Make a dry mount of the mold (see Figure 22). To make a dry mount, use a paper punch to punch a hole in the center of a white index card cut to 1 × 3 inches. Lay the paper on a flat, smooth surface. Affix a piece of clear tape so that it covers the hole. Carefully peel the paper away from the smooth surface. Turn the paper over and sprinkle mold onto the transparent surface. Position the paper slide on the stage so that light will shine through the tape. Use the low-power scanning (4X) objective to begin your examination.

Is it *Penicillium*? If so, then you have isolated the organism that causes moldy orange disease—and demonstrated Koch's postulates.

a)

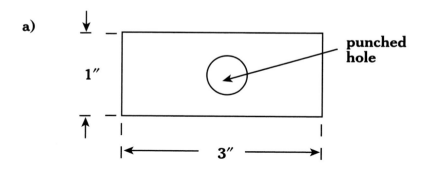

punched hole

1″

3″

b)

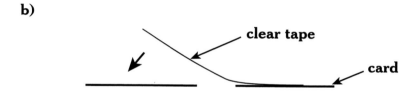

clear tape

card

c)

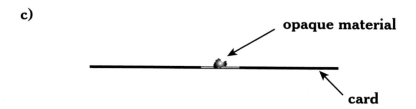

opaque material

card

Figure 22.

MAKING A DRY MOUNT

a) Punch a hole in a 1 in × 3 in index card. b) Cover the hole with a piece of clear tape. c) Sprinkle the mold on the sticky tape surface. Position the hole on the microscope stage so that light can penetrate. Observe the mold under the microscope, beginning at 40X.

Science Project Ideas

- Most microbes need at least 20 percent moisture content to grow. Design experiments that explore this relationship between moisture content and microbial growth. For example, you could place various dry foods inside a moisture chamber (a sealed plastic container containing a damp sponge) to determine at what moisture and temperature levels—measured with a digital relative humidity and temperature probe—mold growth first appears. (Humidity and temperature probes can be obtained at retail electronic stores.) Evaluate various food packaging methods. Are they effective in protecting food inside your moisture chamber?

- Use pH paper to find out which foods are acidic foods—those having a pH below 7.0. **With adult permission**, use a knife to cut through various fruits such as lemons, apples, oranges, pears, grapes, and cherries. Obtain a pH reading by placing the pH paper on the freshly cut surface. Record the pH data in your notebook. Which fruits are the most acidic—that is, have the lowest pH reading? Test vegetables. Are they acidic or basic (pH above 7.0)?

  Expose these cut fruits and vegetables to the air to find out how long it will take for them to mold (spoil). Use "The Microbe Identification Guide" (Appendix A) to determine which microbes (bacteria, yeasts, or molds) prefer acidic foods and which do not.

● Experiment with various foods to see whether any prevent spoilage or kill fungi. Try vinegar, onion or garlic juice, salt, hot pepper, lemon juice, and other foods. Develop your own powerful preserving agent to fight aggressive spoilage microbes.

Investigation 16

What Is the Best Temperature for Leavening Dough?

Materials

✓ **an adult**

✓ dry measuring cup

✓ tablespoon

✓ all-purpose flour

✓ sugar

✓ electronic or kitchen thermometer

✓ mixing bowl

✓ wooden mixing spoon

✓ 1 package active dry yeast

✓ breadboard

✓ 3 clean kitchen cloths

✓ knife

✓ 3 metric rulers

✓ 3 Pyrex® measuring cups

✓ refrigerator

✓ oven (optional)

✓ pot holders (optional)

✓ magnifying glass

In bread making, a leavening agent causes carbon dioxide gas to form in the dough. The carbon dioxide gas cannot escape, so the dough rises. Baking powder (sodium bicarbonate and starch), sour milk, and active dry (baker's) yeast are common leavening agents.

Yeast cells make enzymes that convert sugar into alcohol and carbon dioxide. This process is called fermentation. Let's investigate the best temperature for yeast growth and fermentation to occur in making dough rise.

Most commercial and home bakers make yeast bread using at least four ingredients—flour, water or milk, sugar, and yeast. Although flour provides some of the sugar needed for fermentation, bakers usually add a small amount of pure sugar to hasten the fermentation process.

Measure ½ cup (120 mL) of very warm water in a Pyrex® measuring cup. Add one tablespoon sugar. Use a wooden spoon to mix well. Sprinkle 1 package of active dry yeast over the sugar water. Set aside for about 10 minutes. Note any changes to the yeast that you see.

Measure out 4 ½ cups of all-purpose flour. Put about half the flour (2 ¼ cups) in a mixing bowl, and make a well in the middle. Pour the yeast mixture into the well of flour. Mix together with the wooden spoon. Add the rest of the flour, a little at a time, and continue mixing by hand. When the dough begins to leave the sides of the bowl, remove the dough and place it onto a lightly floured breadboard.

The dough will be slightly sticky. Cover it with a cloth and let it sit for about 10 minutes. Uncover it and knead the dough for at least 5 minutes by continually folding it over on itself and pressing down. Kneading helps develop gluten—a sticky substance that helps the dough stay together as it rises.

Use a knife and a ruler to measure and cut four identical pieces of dough. Record their dimensions in your notebook. Place three of these pieces at the bottom of each of three identical Pyrex® measuring cups. Insert a metric ruler into each of the measuring cups with the scale visible through the side of the cup. Lightly cover each cup with a cloth.

Examine the remaining piece of dough with a magnifying glass. Sketch what you observe in your notebook.

Under adult supervision, place each of the measuring cups of dough in various temperature conditions, ranging from just above freezing to about 150°F (65°C). For example, you might place one cup in a refrigerator (42°F, or 6°C), one at room temperature (70°F, or 21°C) and one in an oven set on Warm (about 140–150°F, or 60–65°C). If an oven is not available, try placing one measuring cup in a cool room (e.g., the basement) and another in a very warm room. Use an instant-read thermometer to take temperatures throughout the experiment, in each location, and record the temperatures in your notebook.

If temperature conditions are favorable, yeast cells will consume the sugar, release carbon dioxide gas, and begin to reproduce (see Figure 22). The more yeast cells reproduce, the faster the fermentation process, and the sooner and higher the bread dough will rise.

Observe the fermentation process by measuring the height to which the dough in each measuring cup rises. Make sure you use pot holders to handle the measuring cup placed in a heated oven. Take readings every half hour, and record them in your notebook. You may even choose to graph your data. Monitor the fermentation process over 3 to 4 hours. Which temperature conditions are optimal for fermentation? Which are detrimental?

Remove the dough pieces and cut them in half with a knife. Observe the cut ends with a magnifying glass. Sketch your observations in your notebook. What are you observing?

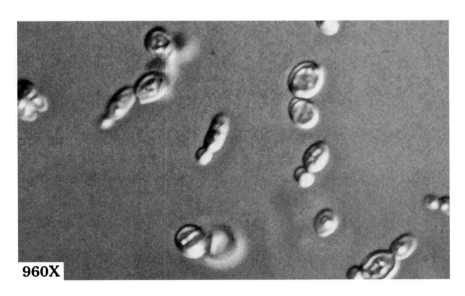

960X

Figure 23.

These yeast cells are shown under high magnification (960X).

When you have finished, throw the dough away. Do not eat the dough you have made.

Science Project Idea

Investigate yeast cell reproduction at the same temperatures you used for rising dough. Make three yeast-sugar solutions by mixing a pinch of active dry yeast in separate cups of sugar water (1 tablespoon of sugar in a cup of bottled water) at room temperature. Place each of the cups in the same three temperature conditions used for the dough rising experiment. Allow the yeast cells to reproduce for 30 minutes. Use an eyedropper to collect a sample of sugar water from each of the three containers. Mix a drop of sugar water with a drop of 0.1% methylene blue stain on a clean microscope slide. **Always wear safety glasses and disposable gloves when using biological stains.** Add a coverslip and observe first under low magnification (40X), and then medium magnification (100X) of a compound microscope.

Make additional microscopic observations of sugar water samples, at half-hour intervals, over a four-hour period. Do the number of yeast cells in a 40X field of view increase over time at a particular temperature? Does your cell growth data agree with your dough rising data?

Chapter 7

Microbes You Know as Protists

They live in pondwater; on submerged rocks, aquarium glass, and bark; in soils and beach sands; even in snow. But you usually cannot see them clearly—except through a microscope. They are protists, microbes usually consisting of one cell or a loose collection of cells (colony). Most are capable of moving—propelled by whiplike flagella, by hairlike cilia, or by cell extensions.

Although most protists are single-celled eukaryotes, they do the same things that other larger organisms do. They eat, make their own food, move, and select partners for reproducing.

Protists include protozoans, algae, slime molds, and seaweeds. They play different roles in their various microhabitats. Some are scavengers, feeding on plant and animal remains. Others feed on bacteria or on other protists. Still others make their own food the way green plants do. Certain protists do a combination of all three.

Investigation 17

What Is in That Puddle?

Materials

- ✓ collection jars with lids
- ✓ resealable plastic bags
- ✓ marker to label sample jars and bags
- ✓ labels
- ✓ eyedropper
- ✓ kitchen baster
- ✓ flat-ended toothpicks
- ✓ pondwater
- ✓ polyethylene oxide
- ✓ teaspoon
- ✓ wooden craft stick
- ✓ microscope slides
- ✓ coverslips
- ✓ compound microscope, with light source
- ✓ liquid measuring cup
- ✓ water

"I looked at it through a microscope and I discovered in this [puddle] water so unbelievably many little animacules . . ."

—Antoni van Leeuwenhoek
June 28, 1713

Leeuwenhoek's "animalcules," or "little animals," were microbes—bacteria, protists, and a variety of other, larger, microlife-forms such as hydras and water fleas. He and other scientists, such as Robert Hooke, spent hours peering at microbes, observing microlife in puddles, mud oozes, gutter sediments and waters, and other familiar locales.

Look for puddles that have a green film on the bottom—a sure sign of a layer of protists. Use a kitchen baster to suck up puddle water and bottom muds and sands for microscopic examination. Be sure to bring small, resealable jars with lids or plastic bags that can be labeled to hold your samples.

Most puddle and pond microbes move quite rapidly. To observe them under a microscope, you will need to add a barrier that will slow them down without harming them. The slowing solution will enable you to view cell movement and internal cell functions more easily. You can make a protist-slowing solution by thoroughly mixing 1 teaspoon of polyethylene oxide (see Appendix C) in 3 ounces (90 mL) of warm water. Stir the mixture continually with a wooden craft stick to make sure all the polyethylene oxide goes into solution. Use a toothpick to pick up a small amount of this solution and transfer it to a clean microscope slide. Then add a drop of pondwater to the protist-slowing solution. Mix the two drops with the toothpick. Add a coverslip to complete the wet mount preparation (see Figure 6).

Examine the preparation first at low magnification (40X), then at higher magnifications (100X and 430X). Be sure to adjust the iris or disc diaphragm to not allow too much light to pass through the sample. Use "The Microbe Identification Guide" (Appendix A) to identify common puddle microlife.

Investigate whether puddles are good habitats for creating microlife communities. What microlife-forms are first observed after a puddle forms? Do these microlife populations change over time? Are there differences between deep and shallow puddles? Between puddles on city streets and puddles in soil or gravel next to a road? If you live in a rural area, do farmland puddles contain different microbes than puddles around your house?

Science Project Ideas

- After the puddle dries up, take a teaspoon sample of surface material from where the puddle was and place it in a baby food jar. Add 1 ounce (30 mL) of bottled water to the surface material sample. Mix the sample thoroughly in the water and allow it to sit on a shelf for a few hours. Use an eyedropper medicine dropper to sample the still water in the jar.

- Take 1 to 3 oz dried soil or sand samples from dried-up puddles. Record the microlife-forms you find in them.

Then place the samples in coil envelopes. Store these samples over the winter. In the spring, add the sample to the bottom of an olive jar, then add 3 to 5 oz of bottled water. Swirl the jar to mix the sample. Then let the puddle sample sit so that the soil settles to the bottom. Use an eyedropper to sample the water and soil grains. Do the same microlife-forms that you recorded again appear?

● Make a micro puddle so that you can examine microlife populations over time. To make one:

1. Roll a piece of silicone culture gum (see Appendix C) or modeling clay into a thin rod approximately 1 inch (2.5 cm) long.

2. Carefully shape this strip into a circle in the center of a clean microscope slide. To avoid leaks, be sure to press down so that the silicone gum (or clay) forms a tight seal.

3. Add a few grains of sand or soil from a dried-up puddle or other source, such as a garden.

4. Using an eyedropper, fill the microaquarium pocket with your collected sample. You may even add tiny pieces of plants collected from around the edges of the puddle.

5. Add a coverslip; avoid creating air bubbles.

View your micro puddle using a low-power objective lens (4X or 10X). Higher magnification objectives are too long and may crack the coverslip while focusing. Be sure to adjust the iris or disc diaphragm to not allow too much light to pass through the micro puddle. The silicone culture gum allows for the transfer of gases, so microbes in your micro puddle can remain alive for weeks.

Make a number of micro puddles using sands and soils from various locations. Use these preparations to study how these environments affect microlife populations. Record your observations over days and weeks. For example, does salting roads affect nearby microlife? **With an adult's permission**, find out if puddles formed near oil or gasoline transfer pumps have different microlife populations than other puddles.

Investigation 18

What Do Microbes Like to Eat?

Materials

- ✓ collection jars and covers
- ✓ labels and marker
- ✓ resealable plastic bags
- ✓ eyedropper
- ✓ polyethylene oxide
- ✓ teaspoon
- ✓ paper cups
- ✓ pondwater or puddle water
- ✓ peppercorns
- ✓ dry cereal
- ✓ dried grass clippings or timothy hay
- ✓ microscope slides
- ✓ coverslips
- ✓ compound microscope, with light source
- ✓ bottled water

Leeuwenhoek made infusions—water broths—of seeds and grasses. He used the infusions to feed microbes. In this investigation you will learn how to identify various microbes and see if your observations agree with those made by Leeuwenhoek (see Table 6).

One common infusion is pepper water. To make a pepper water infusion, fill a small jar two-thirds full with collected pond or puddle water. Add 6 to 8 peppercorns to the jar. Replace the lid loosely on the jar. Allow it to stand in an area that receives indirect sunlight. The sill of a north-facing window is an excellent location. Use an eyedropper to sample its contents over time. Make microscopic observations. Begin by examining wet mount preparations (see Figure 6) at low magnification (40X). Then switch to a higher magnification. You may need to reduce the lighting by using the disc or iris diaphragm to obtain a clearer view. Leeuwenhoek made observations of pepper water over many months.

It is a good idea to always mix a drop of collected water with a drop of protist-slowing solution so that you can easily observe motile microlife-forms. (To make protist-slowing solution, see Investigation 10.)

Use Leeuwenhoek's notes (Table 6) as a guide when examining pepper water. Can you confirm his observations?

Table 6.

LEEUWENHOEK'S OBSERVATION OF PROTISTS IN PEPPER WATER INFUSION

Description	Hint See "The Microbe Identification Guide"	
"I saw a floating . . . a great many green round particles, of the bigness of sand grains."	large ball-shaped colony (protist colony)	
"In structure these little animals were fashioned like a bell, and at the round opening they made such a stir . . . I must have seen quite 20 of these little animals on their long tails . . . yet in an instant, as it were, they pulled in their bodies and tails together."	a ciliate on a stalk	
". . . sort of little animals, . . . were incredibly small; nay so small, in my sight, that I judged that even if 100 of the wee animals lay stretched out one against the other, they could not reach to the length of a grain of sand."	bacteria	
"These were well-nigh round, and their motion was mostly all a-rolling, where-withal they didn't much hur-ray themselves."	small flagellates	
"I saw some which were a good 20 times bigger than the biggest sort spoken of. . . . These were long, and bent crooked, the upper part of the body round, but flat beneath, looking much after the fashion of a peel of a large citron [lemon-shaped fruit]."	a large ciliate with "walking legs"— fused cilia	

In your notebook, draw the organisms you observe. Add notes, just as Leeuwenhoek did, that carefully describe the size, motion, color, and behavior of each particular microbe.

Based on your observations, what can you tell about microbe eating habits? If you sprinkle some small pieces of dry cereal in a jar containing bottled water, what happens over two to three days? Why does the water turn cloudy? Why do bacteria grow? If you were to add several ounces (30 to 90 mL) of a pondwater sample to the jar containing bacteria, what do you think would happen? If you were to make wet mounts of the water in the jar a week after adding pondwater, do you think you would observe protists (e.g., ciliates)? Is the water sample becoming less cloudy? Do you think ciliates eat bacteria?

Make other types of infusions. Place some chopped grass clippings or timothy hay in the bottom of a jar. Add collected or bottled water. Place a lid loosely on top of the jar. Let it stand in indirect light. Sample your infusions over weeks and months.

Science Project Ideas

● Find out which type of infusion material (peppercorns, grass, or hay) is best for growing ciliates.

● **With adult permission**, try boiling a mixture of infusion materials in 2 to 3 cups of water. Then let the mixture cool. Pour it into a canning jar. Add 1 to 2 oz of a collected water sample from a pond or puddle, gutter, or stream. Cover the jar and place it on a windowsill that gets northern light. Use an eyedropper to sample the water at various points (top, middle, and bottom). Make wet mount preparations (Figure 6). Is a boiled infusion better at growing microlife-forms than the unboiled ones you made earlier?

Appendix A:

THE MICROBE IDENTIFICATION GUIDE

How To Identify Bacteria

- Colonies appear as shiny or glistening areas to the eye.
- Cell or cells usually observed at high magnification (>430X) and often require special stains to be clearly seen.
- Cells are spheres, rods, spirals, and filaments and do not have a nucleus.
- Some cells have blue-green pigment seemingly distributed evenly throughout cell; may appear as blue-green strands or colorings on moist surfaces or in water.
- Cells get food from dead organic matter (some parasitic); some produce own food (e.g., photosynthesis).

Go to identification key **Bacteria**, p.115

How To Identify Microfungi

- Colonies appear fuzzy to the eye or look like mushrooms.
- Under the microscope, structures are built from a system of intertwined threads—forming a cottony mass—with various spore-producing reproductive structures (fruiting bodies).
- Cells have one or more nuclei.
- Most forms do not move.
- Cells get food from dead organic matter; some are parasites.

Go to identification key **Microfungi,** p.117

How To Identify Protists

- Most are single cells or groups of cells; generally observed at magnifications below 430X.
- Some cells appear as colored strands or coloring on moist surfaces and in water.
- All cells have nucleus; some have many nuclei.
- Some cells have green pigment contained in tiny sacs (chloroplasts)—pigment is never spread throughout the cell.
- Most cells move about by whiplike flagella, by cilia, or by cell extensions.
- Show great variety in cellular organization: single cells, groups of cells (colony or filament), or multicellular organization (seaweeds).
- Some cells make their own food; some get food from eating others; some absorb nutrient molecules from their surroundings—some can switch from one mode to the other; some are parasitic.

Go to identification key **Protists, p. 118**

To use these keys, begin with statement 1a and proceed until the identification is certain, ending in a microbe group. Then try to identify individual group members in the illustration.

KEY TO BACTERIA

1a The smallest of living cells, most require application of a stain to be clearly observed at high magnifications (>430X). Cells in varied arrangements: single (rods, spirals, spheres, long filaments), in chains, or in small groups . . .
TRUE BACTERIA

Spheres—cocci; usually adhere after division to form clusters of various shapes according to the plane of division of the cells. Types of clusters include: Diplococcus (pairs), Tetracoccus (groups of 4), Streptococcus (chains), Sarcina (cubes of 8), Staphylococcus (irregular clusters).

Rods—bacilli. May be single or adhere end to end to form chains; some produce spores; some have flagella for locomotion.

Spirals—Microspira (short rods slightly bent), spirillum (rigid spirals).

Filaments—colorless, long, multicelluar threads (with or without cross walls); some with slow gliding locomotion.

1b Larger cells are blue-green with pigments seemingly distributed throughout the cell [Cyanobacteria] . . . **go to 2**

2a Overall threadlike (filament) appearance; cells arranged one on top of the other . . .
FILMAMENTOUS CYANOBACTERIA

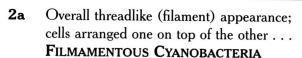

2b Cells distributed within a gelatinous matrix . . .
COCCOID CYANOBACTERIA

BACTERIA YOU MAY SEE		
Organism	**Habitat**	**Size**
Rod-shaped bacteria	All microhabitats	2–7 μm
Spiral-shaped bacteria	All microhabitats	0.8–60 μm
Sphere-shaped bacteria	All microhabitats	0.5–3.5 μm
Bacillus thuringensis	commercial bioinsecticide	0.9–3 μm
Lactobacillus acidophilusdairy	products	0.9–6 μm
Magnetotactic bacteria	marsh muds	2–6 μm
Rhodospirillum	stagnant water and muds exposed to light	2.5–10 μm
Rhizobium	root nodules of leguminous plants (e.g. clover)	9–3 μm
Gloecapsa	mats & films, quiet waters	6–12 μm cell; 2 mm colony
Nostoc	mats & films, quiet waters	5–8 μm cell; 2 cm colony
Anabaena	mats & films, quiet waters	8–10 μm filament diameter
Oscillatoria	mats & films, quiet waters	2–10 μm filament diameter

KEY TO MICROFUNGI

1a Macroscopic fruiting body (mushroom or toad- stool) and associated white cottony or spider web-like filaments . . . **BASIDIOMYCETES**

1b Cottony mass with microscopic fruiting bodies . . . **go to 2**

2a Cottony mass of interconnecting tubelike filaments (hyphae) along with colored spore-carrying organs— microscopic fruiting bodies— on stalks [MOLDS] . . . **go to 3**

2b Does not appear as a cottony mass. Oval- shaped cells, sometimes with one or more buds . . . **YEASTS**

3a Hyphae with cross walls . . . **DEUTEROMYCETES**

3b Hyphae without cross walls . . . **ZYGOMYCETES**

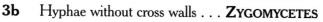

FUNGI YOU MAY SEE

	Organism	Comments	Habitat
	Aspergillus niger	black spore cases; hyphae with cross walls	damp microhabitats
	Aspergillus flavus	yellow-green spore cases; hyphae with cross walls	damp microhabitats
	Rhizopus	black spore cases; hyphae without cross walls	damp microhabitats
	Mucor	black spore cases; hyphae without cross walls	damp microhabitats
	Penicillium	green to bluish-gray spore cases; hyphae with cross walls	damp microhabitats
	Saccharomyces	10 μm cell	beverages, foods, damp microhabitats

KEY TO PROTISTS

1a   Organism attached to a substrate by stalk . . .
      go to 2

1b   Organism without stalk; free-swimming,
      grouped together, floating, or as a filament
      . . . **go to 3**

2a   Stalk supports large, colored (yellow, purple,
      orange) ball or cattail-like structure (sporangium)
      as viewed with hand lens . . . **SLIME MOLDS**

2b   Stalk supports small cell having either
      tentacles or cilia as viewed with a micro-
      scope . . . **go to 11**

3a   White or colorless . . . **go to 7**

3b   Colored . . . **go to 4**

4a   Green;* Cells contain chloroplasts (tiny colored bags
      of green pigment) . . . **go to 5**

4b   Color not green; yellow, orange or white
      gelatinous or net-like mass having
      streaming cytoplasm . . . **SLIME MOLDS**

5a   Overall threadlike or treelike appearance; cells
      arranged either end to end— comprising a fila-
      ment—or in branching filaments like tiny evergreen
      trees (pigment green, not yellow)* . . .
      FILAMENTOUS GREEN PROTISTS

5b   Cells not arranged in filaments . . . **go to 6**

*PITFALLS: Some ciliated and amoeboid protists contain other
symbiotic green protists and thus appear green. Some cells with
chloroplasts also contain red pigment that can mask green color.

6a Single cell or a group of cells with distinct glasslike walls etched with grooves or holes forming delicate patterns (with yellow pigments) . . . **DIATOMS**

6b Single cell, or group of cells, either motile (with flagella) or without motion but without distinct glass-like walls . . . **GREEN PROTISTS**

7a Exhibits definite motion . . . **go to 8**

7b No motion; spherical with radiating spines (axopods) . . . **ACTINOPODS**

8a Slow-creeping . . . **go to 9**

8b Exhibits other motion . . . **go to 10**

9a Cell possesses a shell sometimes made up of small grains of sand; moves about using fingerlike projections (pseudopods) . . . **SHELLED AMOEBAE**

9b Cell naked (no shell); cell moves about using finger-like projections or broad extensions of the cell (pseudopods) . . . **NAKED AMOEBAE**

10a Cell propelled by one or more whiplike flagella . . . **FLAGELLATED PROTISTS**

10b Cell with many hairlike structures (cilia) either in rows covering the entire body, in tufts, or fused to form thicker pointer-like structures (cirri) used as "legs" for walking or swimming . . . **CILIATED PROTISTS**

11a Attached organism(s); cell body with tentacles often seen feeding on small ciliates . . . **SUCTOREANS**

11b Attached organism(s); cell body with hairlike structures (cilia) . . . **STALKED CILIATES**

PROTISTS YOU MAY SEE			
	Organism	**Size**	**Habitat**
	*Actinospherium* (actinopod)	to 1 mm	quiet waters
	Trichophrya (suctorean)	to 250 μm	quiet waters
	Navicula (diatom)	to 250 μm	mats & films, quiet waters
	Synedra (diatom)	140 μm	moving waters, quiet waters, mats & films
	Closterium (green protist)	150 μm	quiet waters, muds & sands
	Arcella (shelled amoeba)	30–100 μm	soils & sands, quiet waters, mats & films
	Amoeba (naked amoeba)	to 600 μm	soils & sands
	Chilomonas (flagellate)	20–40 μm	quiet waters
	Chlamydomonas (green protist)	20 μm	soils & sands, quiet waters, mats & films
	Euglena (green protist)	30–200 μm	soils & sands, mats & films, quiet waters
	Phacus (green protist)	40 μm	quiet waters

	Organism	Size	Habitat
	Peranema (flagellate)	20–70 μm	quiet waters
	Physarum (slime mold)	macroscopic	moist soils
	Blepharisma (ciliate)	180 μm	quiet waters
	Bursaria (ciliate)	to 1mm	quiet waters
	Colpidium (ciliate)	50–70 μm	quiet waters
	Paramecium (ciliate)	200–260 μm	mats & films, quiet waters
	Spirostomum (ciliate)	to 3mm	soils & sands, quiet waters
	Tetrahymena (ciliate)	40–60 μm	quiet waters
	Euplotes	80–110 μm	soils & sands, quiet waters
	Stentor (ciliate)	to 2mm	quiet waters
	Vorticella (stalked ciliate)	50–150 μm	quiet waters
	Volvox (green protist)	colony to 1mm	quiet waters
	Pleodorina (green protist)	colony to 450 μm	quiet waters
	Spirogyra (filament protist)	visible filament	mats & films, quiet waters
	Zygnema (filament protist)	visible filament	mats & films, quiet waters

Appendix B:

MICROSCOPY AND IMAGE PROCESSING

Some investigations in this book require that you have a compound microscope having at least 430X–960X magnification. Most school microscopes are acceptable for use in viewing these small bacteria cells. Ask your teacher for permission to bring in prepared slide smears for you to examine.

Beware of fantastic claims made by some manufacturers about the magnifying power of microscopes available in retail stores. Most times these viewing instruments have inferior lenses and poor illumination systems.

Microscopes described below are available from the sources listed in Appendix C.

BARREL-FOCUS COMPOUND MICROSCOPE

A barrel-focus compound microscope is a basic full-size compound microscope that allows the user to twist the body tube or barrel to focus. Instead of mirrors or electric light sources, this instrument uses a unique light-gathering plastic, positioned under the stage, that concentrates light for reflected or transmitted light illumination—indoors or out. The microscope uses a single objective and eyepiece lens system, generally having a total magnification capability of 20X up to 200X. This is an excellent beginner's microscope for viewing eukaryotic cells.

OTHER COMPOUND MICROSCOPES

Look for a microscope with a 10X eyepiece and a 43X objective lens (96X is preferable). The microscope should have a mirror or internal light source, built-in condenser, and disc diaphragm. Look for one that is 11–14 inches high. Although more expensive than other microscope types, a compound microscope with good optics is an investment for a lifetime of microlife exploration—at any age.

COMPUTER MICROSCOPE

The QX3 computer microscope is capable of examining specimens or objects described in this book ranging from protists (0.25mm / 250 μm) to sand grains or larger objects. The microscope has three magnification lenses—10X, 60X, and 200X.

The software package that accompanies the QX3 microscope controls the microscope and excels in image processing. It also allows users to create video and time-lapse video clips that can be played on a computer. Check to be sure your computer meets the software's minimum system requirements.

IMAGE PROCESSING

Image processing includes taking, editing, and analyzing digital images. You can use a computer microscope, like the QX3, or a flexible educational video camera, like the ClearOne® FlexCam™, to capture video clips or single JPG images. A guidebook to image processing, including activities, is available from the sources listed in Appendix C.

IMAGEJ

ImageJ is a free, public-domain image analysis program developed by the National Institutes of Health (NIH). Because this program is written in Java programming language, it will run on virtually any computer platform. With ImageJ, you can capture images, open files stored on your computer, or even download images from the Internet. Then you can use the many tools offered in the program to measure, count, calculate area, and label an image. You can even animate and create time-lapse movie clips.

The NIH hosts the primary Web site for ImageJ: <http://rsb.info.nih.gov/ij/>. Here you can download the latest version of ImageJ, information, updates, and add-ons (called plug-ins).

OTHER IMAGE PROCESSING PROGRAMS

Most of the following programs are readily available and will allow you to work with digital images: Kodak EasyShare®, ArcSoft PhotoImpression™ and VideoImpression™, and PhotoStudio™.

Appendix C:

SCIENCE SUPPLY COMPANIES

Aldon Corporation
1533 West Henrietta Road
Avon, NY 14414-9409
800-724-9877
http://www.aldon-chem.com

Becker Underwood
1305 South 58th Street
Saint Joseph, MO 64507
800-232-5907
http://www.beckerunderwood.com/

Carolina Biological Supply Company
2700 York Road
Burlington, NC 27215
800-334-5551
http://www.carolina.com

Connecticut Valley Biological Supply Company
82 Valley Road
South Hampton, MA 01703
800-355-6813
http://www.ctvalleybio.com

Delta Education
80 Northwest Boulevard
P.O. Box 3000
Nashua, NH 03061-3000
800-442-5444
http://www.delta-education.com/

Discovery Scope® Inc.
3202 Echo Mountain Drive
Kingwood, TX 77345
http://www.discoveryscope.com

Edmund Scientific
60 Pearce Avenue
Tonawanda, NY 14150
800-728-6999
http://www.scientificsonline.com

Fisher Science Education
485 South Frontage Road
Burr Ridge, IL 60521
800-955-1177
http://www.fisheredu.com

Flinn Scientific
P.O. Box 219
Batavia, IL 60510-0219
800-452-1261
http://www.flinnsci.com

Frey Scientific
P.O. Box 8101
100 Paragon Parkway
Mansfield, OH 44903
800-225-3739
http://www.freyscientific.com

Neo/SCI Corporation
P.O. Box 22729
100 Aviation Avenue
Rochester, NY 14692-2729
800-526-6689
http://www.neosci.com

Science Kit and Boreal Laboratories
777 East Park Drive
Tonawanda, NY 14150
800-828-7777
http://www.sciencekit.com

Further Reading

De Kruif, Paul. *Microbe Hunters*. New York: Harcourt Brace, 2002.

Dyer, Betsey. *A Field Guide to Bacteria*. Ithaca, N.Y.: Cornell University Press, 2003.

Kranmer, Stephen. *Hidden Worlds: Looking Through a Scientist's Microscope*. Boston: Houghton Mifflin, 2001.

Rainis, Kenneth G., and Bruce J. Russell. *Guide to Microlife*. Danbury, Conn.: Franklin Watts, 1996.

————. *Microscope Science Projects and Experiments: Magnifying the Hidden World*. Berkeley Heights, N.J.: Enslow Publishers, Inc., 2003.

Silverstein, Alvin, Virginia Silverstein, and Laura Silverstein Nunn. *Cells*. Brookfield, Conn.: Twenty-First Century Books, 2002.

Internet Addresses

Michigan State University. *Microbe Zoo*. <http://www.commtechlab.msu.edu/sites/dlc-me/zoo/index.html>

Quill Graphics. *Cells Alive!* ©1994-2004. <http://www.cellsalive.com>

The Regents of the University of Michigan. *Science Fair Project Resource Guide*. ©1995-2005. <http://www.ipl.org/div/kidspace/projectguide>

Index